'In *Cracking Social Mobility: How /
Help to Level the Playing Field*, To
proposals on how to tackle social im
that by harnessing the power of tecł
reaches their full potential. For the ____ _
we cannot afford to ignore technology's potential to improve the
delivery of teaching and learning in the classroom. We should grasp
opportunities to ignite innovation, whenever they arise. A must-read
for policymakers in the Department for Education.'

The Rt. Hon. David Davis MP

'AI offers real prospects for significant advance on social mobility
for disadvantaged students, who have been insufficiently helped by
conventional educational approaches. This book addresses a very
important subject.'

Sir Anthony Seldon

'This is an important and timely book. So much of our education
system – its curriculum, its methods of assessment, its attitudes
– seems locked in the past. *Cracking Social Mobility* looks to a
more optimistic future, demonstrating how our most entrenched
societal weakness might finally be overcome through technology,
especially artificial intelligence. Tom Moule's arguments are urgent
and compelling.'

*Geoff Barton, General Secretary of the
Association of School and College Leaders*

'"Social mobility" must have begun to feel like a worn-out aspiration
to vast swathes of the global population. The consequences of our
collective failure to fill this widening gap will be deep and long-
lasting and for the most part we as societies, governments and
citizens are merely sleepwalking into the ramifications. *Cracking
Social Mobility* highlights the very real urgency of this issue but also
(thankfully) suggests some potential road maps for the future, the

most important of which is technological innovation and – vitally – applying it to education it in a way that is beneficial to all.

'Through a series of sincere and passionate arguments, Tom Moule shows us how better adoption of technological innovation can improve equality in education, and how technology can help amplify the efficiency of educators and educational institutions. He suggests a number of ways in which we can close the growing chasm between the world's digitally divided communities to create a sustainable playing field for future generations. When it comes to the social mobility crisis, this book doesn't pretend to have all the answers, but it certainly offers some of them. For anyone thinking about strategic policies to future-proof our global community, Tom's book is a very good place to start.'

Lord David Puttnam

TOM MOULE

CRACKING SOCIAL MOBILITY

How AI and Other Innovations Can Help to
Level the Playing Field

UNIVERSITY OF
BUCKINGHAM
PRESS

Copyright © Tom Moule 2021

All rights reserved. No reproduction, copy or transmission of this publication may be made without written permission.

Except for the quotation of short passages for the purposes of research or private study, or criticism and review, no part of this publication may be reproduced, stored in a retrieval system, copied or transmitted, in any form or by any means, electronic, mechanical, photocopying, recording or otherwise, now known or hereafter invented, save with written permission or in accordance with the provisions of the Copyright, Design and Patents Act 1988, or under terms of any licence permitting limited copying issued by the publisher.

This book is sold subject to the condition that it shall not, by way of trade or otherwise, be lent, resold, hired out, or otherwise circulated without the publisher's prior consent in any form of binding or cover other than that in which it is published and without a similar condition including this condition being imposed on the subsequent purchaser.

Any person who does any unauthorised act in relation to this publication may be liable to criminal prosecution and civil claims for damages.

ISBN 978-1-80031-5-624

CONTENTS

INTRODUCTION

The public mood is sour, sometimes angry. Whole tracts of Britain feel left behind. Whole communities feel the benefits of globalisation have passed them by. Whole sections of society feel they are not getting a fair chance to succeed. The growing sense that we have become an us-and-them society is deeply corrosive of our cohesion as a nation. There is a mood for change in Britain.

Alan Milburn, former Chair of the Social Mobility Commission, writing in the foreword to *Time For Change: An Assessment of Government Policies on Social Mobility 1997-2017*, The Social Mobility Commission.[1]

The term 'AI winter' refers to a period of stagnation during which the advancement of artificial intelligence grinds to a halt and widespread despondency creeps in. The world is not currently undergoing an AI winter; that said, the period we are now enduring could aptly be described as a social mobility winter. At the current glacial rate of progress it will take more than forty years to bridge the developmental gaps between less well-off and more advantaged five-year-olds,[2] eighty years will pass before people of all socioeconomic backgrounds achieve equal access to university;[3] and if things carry on as they are, a century from now we may finally see the eradication of the educational attainment gap at sixteen between those who were born into poorer households and those who were born into richer ones.[4]

A sense of helplessness accompanies this inertia. Polling conducted by the Social Mobility Commission in 2019 demonstrated that 44% of people believe that your successes in life are 'mainly determined by your background and who your parents were'[5] rather than by how hard you work. The same poll showed that 39% of people felt that it was becoming harder to climb the social ladder, compared to just 22% who felt it was becoming easier. Equally disheartening is that efforts to mount a resurgence have often been deprioritised by those in power. In December 2017, Alan Milburn, then chair of the Social Mobility Commission, resigned from his post, citing that the government lacked the 'necessary bandwidth to ensure that the rhetoric of healing social division is matched with the reality'.[6] Despite lip service being routinely paid to the social mobility cause, there is often little reason to think that we as a society will emerge from this wintry haze anytime soon.

This inclement climate is a cradle for discord and despair. Some benefit from the opportunities that confer greater life chances; others don't. The latter group feels justifiably aggrieved. Klaus Schwab of the World Economic Forum has warned of the dire consequences of such aggrievements, emphasising that entrenched societal divisions are giving rise to:

> …a growing sense of unfairness, precarity, perceived loss of identity and dignity, weakening social fabric, eroding trust in institutions, disenchantment with political processes, and an erosion of the social contract.[7]

Others have suggested that this profound frustration lies at the heart of the political volatility experienced during recent years.[8] Among these, Sir Michael Wilshaw, former head of

Ofsted, the inspectorate for state schools in England, has argued that the 'malaise' born out of the disenchantment felt by families whose children have had an unfair deal is partly to explain for the result of the EU referendum.[9] A red flag is clearly waving. If we as a society cannot spring ourselves out of this malaise, then this social discord could spiral out of control. Such inequities cannot continue indefinitely. At some point the frost must thaw. But, as I write, we may actually be regressing into a bleaker state of winter.

The impacts of the Covid-19 pandemic on social mobility have not been the primary concern; that said, there are warning signs that the life chances of the least privileged could suffer disproportionately. There are clear indications that the limited provision from nurseries and schools during lockdown has exacerbated existing educational inequalities in the short term. The prolonged period of economic hardship that threatens to follow could leave the less privileged further behind in the long term.[10]

At least during these difficult times some small consolation can be gained from the renewed zeal with which many long-standing societal ills are being grappled. The suffering of victims of domestic violence, the plight of the precarious workforce and the rejection of invaluable members of society who happen to have not been born in this country, are starting to be given warranted levels of attention. Let's hope that in the aftermath of our darkest hour, the concern and compassion that once shone through manages to translate into tangible outcomes. In this spirit, we should seize the chance to resolve the deep-rooted inequalities of opportunity that have plagued our society for so long. It's time to awaken from this state of hibernation and allow all people, from all backgrounds, to blossom.

Any strategy for exiting society's social mobility winter must be centred on practical solutions. Prospective ways forward will come in many shapes and sizes. Wide-reaching reforms will be needed, and so too will highly focused programmes. My intention here is not to provide an overview of the full spectrum of approaches that could be taken. Instead, my aim is to make the case that technologies can help level the playing field when they are purposefully utilised. But demonstrating the role that technology has to play in this endeavour is not my only intention. I am equally eager to make the case for why social mobility needs to be boosted in the first place. In the first chapter, therefore, I argue with vehemence that social mobility should be seen as a moral imperative and a goal towards which societies should strive.

Before continuing any further, however, let's first get to grips with the term 'social mobility'. There are two distinct concepts here: absolute social mobility and relative social mobility.[11] Absolute social mobility is linked to how well one generation does economically compared to the next. Wholescale increases in economic prosperity are a key driver of rising levels of absolute social mobility. In the years following the second world war, for instance, there was a significant expansion of middle-class jobs, meaning that many people born into working-class families were able to advance economically.[12] These people could be said to have risen with their class,[13] which is certainly a positive thing, but if every single person rises with their class, those who start at the bottom of society are still likely to end up in the same relative position. Likewise, those who were born into privilege are likely to maintain their privilege, irrespective of whether this is merited or not. This is where the concept of relative social mobility comes in.

Relative social mobility is about the extent to which an individual's life chances – which can be inferred by the socioeconomic status and level of income they achieve – are determined by their circumstances at birth. The higher a society's levels of relative social mobility, the less relevant your background is to your future successes. The concept of relative social mobility is therefore intrinsically interwoven with that of equality of opportunity. Relative social mobility is what we see, what we can observe and measure when a society distributes opportunity fairly. Equality of opportunity in: relative social mobility out. The analogy I like to draw upon stems from biological inheritance (somewhat ironically). The genotype and the phenotype are two closely linked concepts in genetics. The genotype refers to an organism's underlying genetic information. The phenotype is the observable characteristics that the genetic information gives rise to. To give a simplistic example, the set of genes that give rise to brown eyes are the genotype; the brown eyes themselves are the phenotype. In our case, low levels of relative social mobility are the phenotype, the property we can observe and measure. Inequality of opportunity is the genotype that codes unfairness and unfulfilled potential into the DNA of our society.

I must assert here that anaemic levels of relative social mobility (which I refer to as social immobility) is not the only social phenomena that arises from inequalities of opportunity. The gender divide and racial inequality are two societal problems that urgently need to be resolved. These problems are also related to fundamental inequalities of opportunity. And while they are not the focus of this book, which has social immobility squarely in its cross hairs, these problems are equally profound.

At a moral level, relative social mobility is a far more engrossing concept than absolute social mobility. Relative social mobility is about ensuring an individual's life chances are not limited or adversely affected by matters beyond their control. It is concerned with the undue influence that a person's socioeconomic background has on the opportunities available to them and the destinations they are likely to reach. Absolute social mobility, on the other hand, is concerned with ever-increasing levels of opportunity, but without respect to which groups of people are most likely to enjoy the benefits that these opportunities bring. It is self-evident that increasing the level of opportunities on offer is a good thing. Indeed, I doubt that anyone would be openly against absolute social mobility. But the concept of absolute social mobility does not help address the matter of how opportunities are spread throughout a society. The concept of relative social mobility, on the other hand, does. From here on in, therefore, wherever I refer to 'social mobility' please read this as 'relative social mobility'.

We must combat entrenched inequalities of opportunity if we are to boost social mobility. Technology has much to offer here. In Chapter 2 I will outline the fundamental aptitudes of technology that can be utilised to level the playing field. As we'll see, by automating and augmenting human labour, technologies can increase the productivity and efficiency of educational institutions and make developmental opportunities both more affordable and more readily available. By extracting insights from data, technologies can improve teaching and learning, and enable fairer decisions to be made at critical junctures. And by connecting people to each other and expanding their horizons, technologies can equalise social capital. This chapter looks at these fundamental aptitudes of technology under the microscope and explains why they have the potential to equalise opportunity. During subsequent chapters we will then see how these aptitudes can be mobilised in practice in order to achieve a more equitable distribution of opportunities throughout society.

In Chapter 3, I'll demonstrate that affordable, highly advanced innovations will radically disrupt the private tuition market, meaning that young people's access to supplementary opportunities outside of school needn't be dependent on their family having a relatively large disposable income. In Chapter 4, I'll show how educational divides within the school system could be narrowed significantly. And in Chapter 5,

I will explore the innovations that could be harnessed to enable people of all backgrounds to identify, work towards, and secure a career that they find fulfilling. In Chapter 6, I'll show that technologies have further roles to play in addressing disparities in early years development and in access to post-18 educational opportunities; I'll also discuss why innovative alternatives to high-stakes assessments could be a boon for social mobility.

I acknowledge, however, that in the current climate, there may be misgivings around my optimism. If technology is set to be the great leveller of opportunity, why aren't educational divides narrowing at a time when digital learning is being so intensively relied upon?

The first and most obvious point to make is that remote learning is not representative of the true potential of educational technology. As I will demonstrate throughout this book, technology can amplify the skill sets of educators, enhance established pedagogical practices, and increase the efficiency of educational institutions. Just as technology acted as a much-needed safety net while schools were closed, it will serve as a springboard in the new normal if embedded within schools, colleges and universities that are well equipped to harness its capacities with purpose.

We should also consider that when the crisis struck, some of the most advanced technologies for learning were not yet in widespread use. Both the development and the uptake of artificial intelligence and virtual reality in education, for instance, had been accelerating, but neither of these technologies had become ubiquitous. Learning in lockdown may have been markedly different if this new generation of innovations had reached sufficient levels of ubiquity before the crisis. On this point, in an article entitled *Coronavirus and the future of learning: What AI could have made possible*, Stéphan Vincent-Lancrin of the Organisation for Economic Co-operation and Development (OECD) explained that learners could have benefited during lockdown had the use of AI in education been more prevalant.[14]

Finally, and most importantly, the pandemic has also exposed the brutality of the digital divide. Looking at differences between individual students in the UK, those in the most deprived schools were significantly more likely to lack sufficient access to a device on which to learn from home.[15] This divide at an individual level has also been mirrored at an institutional level, as shown by the following finding from the Sutton Trust: '60% of private schools and 37% of state schools in the most affluent areas already had an online platform in place to receive work, compared to 23% of the most deprived schools'.[16] Together, these patterns may partly explain why children from wealthier households spent on average 30% more time learning from home than children from less well-off households during lockdown.[17]

The digital divide presents a mortal risk to social mobility. We have learned this the hard way. That said, the digital divide is not inevitable. In Chapter 8, I outline how this divide can be addressed head-on so that all people can enjoy the impending educational upgrade.

Before then, in Chapter 7, I address another prickly issue. The economic tremors caused by technological disruption may well result in fewer opportunities for all, creating particularly severe disadvantages for those from less privileged backgrounds. While, at a strategic level, the world must rise to the challenge of enabling inclusive growth in the digital economy, I'll show that at a tactical level, technological solutions may be of great service in maintaining equitable opportunities in an increasingly digital world.

In Chapter 9 I explain where and why technology does not provide a means of addressing inequality of opportunity. In many cases, technology can break the shackles that bind a person's life chances to their socioeconomic background. But in other cases, these shackles are invulnerable to technology's might. My intention in this chapter is not to enfeeble the case for technology. All utilities have their limitations. Indeed, understanding the limitations of advanced technologies enables us to focus on how they can be harnessed optimally. That said, I am keen to stress that technological innovation is not the sole answer to addressing social immobility. If the conditions are right, technology can expand opportunities immeasurably and equitably. But what if the conditions are not right? What about those young people who endure the unendurable every day of their lives? Technology will play a role in boosting their life chances to some extent, but alone it may be woefully insufficient. Unless we also address these people's most fundamental needs, their wings will remain clipped.

Cumulatively, throughout this book I hope to convince readers of two things:

- First, that social immobility cannot be tolerated. A person's life chances should not be fixed, limited, steered or unfairly influenced by the circumstances into which they were born;[18] as such, improved social mobility is a goal towards which societies should strive.

- And second, that by harnessing advanced technologies, we can make strides towards this goal.

While I do not provide a detailed implementation plan within these pages, I hope that this book will motivate action and, in its own right, play some small part in levelling the playing field.

CHAPTER 1

THE CASE FOR SOCIAL MOBILITY

Which of the following claims sounds more alarming to you?

A) You live in a country with an intergenerational earnings elasticity of 0.5.

Or

B) You live in a country in which the grand total of all your hard work, the talents you have honed and the grit you have shown along the way, have the same influence on what you earn in your adult life as does the amount your parents earned when you were a child.

I am going to assume that for most people, the answer is 'B'. While 'A' is just an innocuous statistic, 'B' most certainly is not. It asserts that individuals have limited control over their own destinies. It implies that the outcome of your life is not entirely in your own hands but is significantly influenced by the circumstances into which you were born. And now for the punchline – 'A' and 'B' claim the same thing.

Intergenerational earnings elasticity (or IGE for short) is a measure of how much someone's income is influenced by that of their parents. More importantly, however, it also serves as a proxy for how much control members of a particular society have over their own lives. If you lived in a country with an IGE of 1, you would inevitably earn the same as your parents earned (in real terms). All your friends would earn the same as their parents did. And your children – you guessed it – would end up earning the same amount as you (and as their grandparents, for that matter). Fortunately, no country actually has an IGE of 1, but if such a country did exist, its citizens would effectively have no power to determine their successes in life. At the other extreme is an equally fictitious country with an IGE of zero. Here, your parentage would neither help nor hinder you in the slightest: your successes would be entirely in your own hands.[1]

If you live in the UK or the USA, however, the situation is almost slap bang in the middle of these two extremes. Authoritative studies have reported that both countries have IGEs in the region of 0.5[2] (see figure 1), which suggests that in these countries, your efforts have around the same impact on how much you earn as your parents' income does.[3]

Of course, income is far from a perfect measure of how happy and fulfilled people are in their lives, which is what really matters. But in countries with high IGEs, the reason a person's income is so closely linked to that of their parents is because the whole trajectory of their lives is being directed by their starting point at birth; the closer the IGE gets to 1, the tighter individuals are steered along their forecasted paths. In that imagined country with an IGE of 1, a person's income relative to his or her fellow citizens is predetermined at birth. If you lived in this society, you would have to live with the fact that the quality of your education, your career choices and your chances of career progression were set in stone from day one.[4] While this might sound attractive to those at the top of society – those who have everything to lose, but zero chance of doing so – think on this: in a society with an IGE of 1, every success in life is down to the lottery of birth. Merit has no part to play. The rich, the poor and those in between would be united in their impotence to determine the course of their own lives. In other words, extreme inequality of opportunity is tantamount to fate. When individuals have no control over their own lives the power of destiny is absolute.

In the real world, things aren't quite that bad. France has an IGE of just above 0.4, Germany just above 0.3 and Canada just under 0.2. But even these figures are not something to celebrate. In these countries, intergenerational elasticity is significantly above zero because the direction of people's lives is, to some extent, dictated by their circumstances at birth.

Moving from the abstract to the concrete, the evidence that the playing field is far from level is all around us. The Social Mobility Commission's *State of The Nation Report (2018-19)* revealed that people from better-off backgrounds are 80% more likely to 'make it into' a professional job than people from less well-off backgrounds. This disparity contributes to the overall 'class pay gap' of 24%.[5] To make matters worse, people from less privileged backgrounds are far more likely to be among the lowest paid workers in society – 27% of adults from working class backgrounds earn less than the living wage, which compares to 17% of those from more privileged beginnings. And disadvantaged children are more likely to be unemployed in adult life.[6]

Young people who are not from privileged backgrounds face significant barriers to achieving their full potential. Wealthier applicants are around six times more likely to gain a place at the most selective universities compared to applicants from less privileged backgrounds; a child eligible for free school meals has only a 0.05% chance of gaining a place at Oxbridge.[7] Alas, the problem is not isolated to universities. This divide is mirrored in access to top apprenticeships too, with the Social Mobility Commission showing that people from poorer backgrounds are more likely to be found in 'lower returning' and 'lower level' apprenticeships.[8] Even when the causeways to success are diversified, they can still be dominated by more privileged groups.

These examples give a sense of the disproportionate levels of resistance faced by the most disadvantaged in society. But the negative effects of social immobility are not felt by this group alone. The middle classes feel the pains of inequality of opportunity too.

Only 7% of people in Britain are privately educated[9] – partly due to the fact that average fees are now reported to be as much as £17,000 per year[10] – yet those who were privately educated dominate the most prestigious positions in society. 65% of senior judges were privately educated, as were 59% of the most senior civil servants, 57% of members of the House of Lords, 52% of diplomats and 44% of newspaper columnists.[11] Research has also shown that people who were state-educated are likely to earn around £200,000 less between the ages of twenty-six and forty-two than those who were privately educated.[12] The gap between this privileged group and the rest of society can also be seen at an earlier age. Researchers from Durham University found that being educated privately increases pupils' grades by just under two-thirds on average per subject (i.e. BBB would increase to AAB) even when prior attainment is taken into account.[13] Elsewhere, the Sutton Trust has demonstrated that privately educated students are twice as likely to gain a place at a Russell Group university and seven times as likely to get into Oxford or Cambridge.[14] Ultimately, this means that people from comfortable backgrounds are not immune to diminished life chances, particularly if there is entrenched privilege further up ahead.

These patterns have not arisen by chance; they reflect a fundamental asymmetry in the life chances of people from different backgrounds. But despite the overwhelming evidence that there is a problem with social immobility and inequality of opportunity, there still isn't unanimous agreement that these problems are worth solving. Some view efforts to improve social mobility as an affront to the pursuit of social justice. This group often paints social mobility and equality of opportunity as ingredients of a dog-eat-dog agenda, rather than as a means to achieve fair and equitable outcomes for the many (individuals from all socioeconomic backgrounds) and not the few (those with the resources to unfairly maintain their positions at the top of society).

Others perceive inequality of opportunity as an acceptable by-product of a free society. Of course all parents want the best for their children, and of course those with means will use their resources to support their families. Isn't that the primary duty of parents and guardians, to help secure the best life for their children? So on this basis, is social immobility not a necessary evil?

The problem with both of these concerns is that they rely on misunderstandings of what social mobility is and of how it can be achieved. The arguments are pitched as 'social mobility vs equality' and 'inequality of opportunity vs freedom', even though these clashes are non-existent and avoidable, respectively. Throughout this book, it will become clear that addressing social mobility does not necessitate intrusions upon individual freedoms. Momentarily, by interrogating the concept of inequality of opportunity in greater depth, we'll see that equality of opportunity is a) a goal worth striving towards, and b) not at odds with absolute equality.

When trying to answer questions like 'Is inequality of opportunity acceptable?' or 'Should we strive to live in a more socially mobile society?', it is important to be impartial. Focusing too much on how we are individually affected by social mobility and equality of opportunity could cloud our judgements. To help us achieve this ambitious level of impartiality, let's invoke a thought experiment. John Rawls, a prominent 20th-century philosopher, considered that when trying to determine whether a particular state of affairs is fair or not, people should remove their own circumstances and traits from consideration by imagining themselves standing behind a veil of ignorance and judging a moral issue objectively. From behind the veil, you would have no clue as to your ethnicity, gender, physical health, mental health, sexual orientation, socioeconomic background or indeed any personal factor that might affect the outcomes of your life. From this standpoint, you could hypothetically gaze upon a society – real or imagined – and pass judgement on whether it was fair or not. Your judgement would not be tainted by self-interest; absolute impartiality means there are no interested parties behind the veil.

Equipped with the blissful ignorance provided by the veil, we can now start to examine how fair social immobility and inequality of opportunity are. Behind veil number one is a society with high social immobility. If you were to enter this world at the top of society, you would be fast-tracked to success. You would go to the best schools (and preschools/ nurseries), you would get additional support from the best private tutors, you would get the best support with applying to universities or apprenticeships and you may even be lucky enough to have a job lined up with a friend of the family when you finish. A pretty attractive deal. But the catch is that if you don't enter this world at the top, but start towards the bottom, then a very different fate is in store for you. You may find your life chances diminished by a poorer quality of education, low expectations, lack of advice and guidance on life choices and a job market that is rigged in favour of those with the right connections.

Behind veil number two, however, is a society in which opportunity is distributed equally. No matter what circumstances you were born into, you would have the same opportunities to develop your abilities and convert them into concrete successes. In this society, all people get the same high quality of education, they all have access to equal levels of support in progressing from education into a fulfilling job and they are able to make further progress based on merit alone. In this world, your chances of fulfilling your potential are not affected by your starting point in the slightest; what you make of your life is very much up to you.

So the question is this: if you had no idea what circumstances you were going to be born into, would you choose to enter the world behind veil number one or the world behind veil number two? If you're considering going for number one, be sure to assess whether the risk of being trapped towards the bottom of society would be worth the rewards of being able to coast at the top.

I am strongly of the opinion that the society behind veil number one is thoroughly undesirable. It is unjustifiable that some people, by virtue of their heritage, should have a far greater chance of fulfilling their potential in life, and that others should face a disproportionate number of barriers to fulfilling theirs. We only live one life, so every individual, regardless of their gender, ethnicity, socioeconomic background and a whole host of other factors, should be able to live life to its fullest. As such, equality of opportunity should be the default. Social mobility should be the default. Social immobility is an aberration caused by the fact that people's socioeconomic beginnings have an undue influence on their life chances. Thomas Jefferson famously wrote that it is self-evident that all men are created equal, and that they are all equally endowed with the inalienable right to pursue happiness in their own lives. But if we are willing to tolerate high levels of social immobility, then we are accepting that people (that's all people, not just males) are not created equal, and that many people's circumstances alienate them from, and make ever more nebulous, the right to pursue happiness.

John Rawls himself derived a justification for equality of opportunity from the principles underpinning the veil of ignorance. Hs position was that, 'Those who have the same level of talent and ability and the same willingness to use those gifts should have the same prospects of success regardless of their social class of origin.'[15] While I firmly agree with this, I would clarify that 'talent' and 'ability' should not be interpreted as 'gifts' possessed by the chosen few. Everyone has genuine talents that can enable them to thrive; but only in a society with equality of opportunity will all people be able to develop and convert their talents to the same extent.

You'll have noticed in the examples above, that I didn't explicitly state what the absolute levels of equality were behind the two veils. It could have been that behind veil number one was a highly stratified society but one that had relatively low levels of inequality; while the society behind veil number two could have been highly unequal despite being much more socially mobile. Then again, the first society could have been both more unequal and more immobile; and the second society could have been the polar opposite.

In short, how equal a society is is a different issue from how socially mobile it is, in much the same way that gender equality and absolute levels of equality are two different issues. To illustrate, inequality in the UK rose significantly throughout the 1980s; in 1979 the Gini coefficient (a widely recognised measure of a nation's inequality) was 0.25, but by 1991 it was 0.34.[16] But during the same time period, gender inequality decreased, as demonstrated by the decrease in the gender pay gap from 28.7 to 22.2 per cent.[17]

Now you might think the rise in absolute inequality is a bad thing or you might see it as a good thing; you might not care either way. But I am going to assume that most people are glad that gender equality is increasing – even if they don't think it is increasing quickly enough – because it is self-evidently unfair that men should systematically earn more than women. This is how we should think about social mobility and equality. Regardless of how equal or unequal a society is, it can never be acceptable for people's life chances to be limited by factors beyond their control, such as their sex or the socioeconomic circumstances into which they were born. In some cases, the comparison between gender inequality and social immobility is quite striking. Teach First has cited figures showing that graduates from low-income backgrounds earn on average 10% less than graduates from wealthier backgrounds who are qualified to the same level.[18] In parallel to this pay gap of 10%, there is now also an average gender pay gap among full-time employees of just under 10% (8.6% to be exact).[19] Surely, we can all agree that the latter pay gap is simply unfair. It is self-evidently wrong for women to face greater barriers and have fewer opportunities than men. Remaining faithful to this line of reasoning, while people may have different opinions on equality and inequality, we should all be able to agree that it is wrong for people from less privileged backgrounds to systematically face greater barriers and have fewer opportunities than those from wealthy backgrounds. Both of these pay gaps are equally inequitable.

But in practice wouldn't it be better to focus on inequality?

Inequality of opportunity and inequality are distinct issues in principle. That said, I do acknowledge that they are intertwined in practice. This may add weight to the argument that addressing inequality is important in its own right, but it adds no weight to arguments that social mobility is not a goal worth striving towards. The interconnection between inequality and social immobility certainly does not justify neglecting grotesque inequalities of opportunity.

Looking closer at this relationship, in their highly influential book, *The Spirit Level*, Richard Wilkinson and Kate Pickett note that how socially mobile a country is is strongly linked to how equal that country is.[20] Meanwhile, the Great Gatsby

Curve[21] has frequently been used to demonstrate that there is a reasonably strong correlation between these two factors. Below is a version of this graph, showing the relationship between social immobility (measured using IGE) and inequality (measured using the Gini coefficient).

IGE vs. Gini index

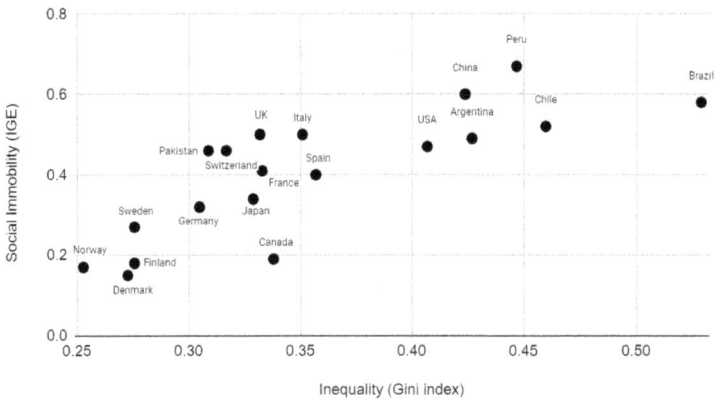

Figure 1[22]

Looking at the graph, we can see that Denmark is near the bottom left-hand corner, meaning it has low inequality and high social mobility (or low social immobility). At the other extreme, countries like Brazil, Chile and Peru have high inequality and low social mobility. This relationship might stir those who object to the pursuits of equality of opportunity and social mobility to point out that if these measures are closely linked to absolute equality, then why shouldn't we put all our might into addressing inequality?

There is no sense denying that these two factors are linked. But this does not mean that the only way to boost social mobility is to decrease inequality. As the graph shows, levels of absolute inequality are very similar in France and Canada, but despite this France's IGE is more than double that of Canada. In these countries wealth is distributed in a similar way but opportunity most certainly is not. We should also not dismiss the possibility that directly boosting social mobility could be a means of achieving greater levels of equality. Indeed, the World Economic Forum has argued that 'low social mobility is both a cause and a consequence of rising inequalities'.[23]

In my view, however, the best argument against the claim that we should sideline the social mobility agenda and instead focus solely on inequality stems from practicalities rather than principles. In practice, abandoning the social mobility agenda would not look like a triumph for social justice. Not one bit. It would mean ignoring targeted policies and programmes that attempt to remedy the fact that poorer children are less likely to go to the best schools. Focused policies that aim to diversify the intakes of universities and apprenticeships – including the most prestigious – to make them more representative of wider society would be hard to justify. Approaches that enable all children to be ready for school and able to make the most of their education might even be frowned upon. Why bother devising targeted solutions to isolated problems, when macroscopically decreasing inequality will solve all our problems at once?

Boosting social mobility will require targeted solutions. As Lee Elliot Major and Stephen Machin note during a discussion on inequality and social immobility in their book *Social Mobility and Its Enemies*, richer parents can utilise their resources to help their children get into the best schools and universities, and to provide them with support from the best private tutors. As a result, education acts as 'the vehicle through which inequality of income drives inequality of opportunities'.[24] If, as a society, we wish to achieve greater levels of social mobility, we must combat such structural inequalities of opportunity decisively and directly. Absolute inequality is without doubt a factor, but that does not mean that direct efforts to address inequality of opportunity should be dismissed.

But isn't social mobility a divisive, unjust agenda?

More forceful opponents of social mobility have claimed that it merely represents an agenda to help a few gifted people climb the ladder, while many others are left behind. This is not a characterisation of social mobility that I recognise. I do, however, accept that social mobility has often been conflated with a more divisive, 'diamond in the rough' agenda, for which policies are only designed to improve the life chances of a small number of people from disadvantaged backgrounds, often at the expense of a great many.

But the vision of social mobility that I am advocating has nothing to do with scavenging for a few diamonds in the rough. The key to achieving this vision is addressing the fact that people's life chances are so often fixed, steered or otherwise unfairly influenced by their socioeconomic circumstances. To achieve social mobility we must combat deep-rooted inequalities; airlifting a few fortunate souls out of disadvantaged circumstances is an inadequate response to entrenched asymmetries in people's life chances.

Let's not forget, in a society with ultra-high levels of social immobility you would have a pretty good chance of predicting how much a child would earn later in life just by looking at their parents' income. That this means underprivileged people are less likely to develop to their full potential is not the only reason that this frustrates me. I am also frustrated because if you can readily predict a child's success in later life without knowing much at all about their character, their motivations, their interests, their dreams and their aspirations, then there is something desperately wrong with the society in which that child lives.

A person's life chances shouldn't depend upon their circumstances at birth: simple. To put it mathematically, if our parents' incomes and social status had no bearing at all on our outcomes in life then everyone would have a 20% chance of reaching the top quintile (the top 20%), a 20% chance of reaching the 2nd quintile, a 20% chance of reaching the 3rd quintile… .and so on.[25] This could perhaps be termed the 20:20 vision of social mobility. Unfortunately, in countries like the UK we are nowhere near observing social mobility with this level of clarity.

As discussed in *Social Mobility and Its Enemies,* intergenerational mobility data from the 1970 birth cohort provides a detailed picture of how far away we are. Looking at young people born into the poorest fifth of households, 35% remained in the poorest quintile, 26% made it to the second-poorest quintile, 23% to the third-poorest quintile; 14% made it to the second-richest band, but only 10% made it all the way into the richest fifth of households. Compare this to the situation for those who were born into the richest fifth. Only 8% of these people ended up in the poorest quintile. 13%, 15% and 23% ended up in the next three quintiles, respectively. And a whopping 41% remained in the richest quintile: four times the rate at which people from the bottom fifth made it into this bracket. Noteworthy too is that those who started in the poorest fifth of households were approximately four times as likely to be there as adults, compared to those who began in the richest fifth of households. But social mobility is not just about the inequalities between the top and the bottom rungs of society. If you were born into the second or third-richest quintiles, you would have around half the chance of making it into the top fifth of households in adult life as those who started in the richest quintile – and you would be almost doubly likely to be in the poorest quintile as them.

Within this 20:20 vision of social mobility there will always be a top quintile that only 20% of people will be in at any one time, but that does not mean that the aim of social mobility is to cherry pick 'the best' and forget about 'the rest'. The 20:20 vision of social mobility will only be achieved when equality of opportunity is optimised. That means removing the barriers to success that disproportionately affect those from more disadvantaged backgrounds; it means making education fairer by ensuring that all experience the same level of excellence, and it means removing unfair advantages conferred by social capital, being linked up in the right networks and having the ability to pay for better and more plentiful developmental opportunities. It most certainly does not mean a tunnel-visioned focus on fast-tracking a small number of people from the bottom of society to the top. Although, as per our 20:20 vision, we should expect 20% of people born into the lowest quintile to ascend to the highest quintile. In concrete terms, this would mean that intakes of the most competitive universities, apprenticeships and professions would become fully representative of wider society.

But won't achieving social mobility require encroachments upon people's freedoms?

Coming from the other end of the ideological spectrum, there is also the objection that any pursuit of equality of opportunity would infringe upon an individual's fundamental freedom to do the best they can for their own children. We know that parents reading to their kids and helping them learn in their early years can initiate divides in the life chances of young people. When parents do what they can to ensure their children go to good schools – where they will be happy and able to thrive – these divides become wider still. And while nepotism is to be frowned upon, parents have a right to provide career advice and guidance to their children to enable them to achieve fulfilment in later life – a practice that is likely to perpetuate social immobility. Equality of opportunity and its corollary – social mobility – are morally desirable goals towards which we should strive. But there seems to be a snag: the fundamental role of parents and families. This may look like a catch-22 situation, but it really isn't.

In the coming chapters I will outline solutions to a number of pain points for social mobility. What should become abundantly clear is that none of these solutions encroach upon personal choice and people's natural predispositions. The key to vanquishing social mobility lies in blowing wide open the avenues of opportunity that are currently dominated by society's 'haves'. Technology is among our most powerful allies in achieving this.

The underlying argument that I have made in this chapter – that social mobility is morally desirable because a person's life chances should not be determined or unfairly influenced by their socioeconomic circumstances at birth – will percolate throughout the book. The key points to take stock of at this juncture, however, are as follows:

- Without high levels of social mobility, the control that individuals have over their own lives is critically limited. If a significant portion of a person's success in life can be explained by their parents' income,[26] then the impact of their talents, grit and work ethic are diluted to an intolerable extent.

- As per John Rawls' reasoning, the unfairness of social immobility is particularly evident when we invoke the veil of ignorance thought experiment. If you had no way of knowing what socioeconomic group you would be born into, would you really opt to live in a society where your life chances could be severely diminished if you were born into less privileged circumstances? Or would you rather live in a society where people from all backgrounds had an equal chance at thriving?

- Social mobility is neither at odds with absolute equality nor in tension with individual freedoms (a point that will be demonstrated throughout this book). As such, a person's views on the moral basis for social mobility should not be affected at all by their perspectives on either of these two issues.

CHAPTER 2

THE CASE FOR TECHNOLOGY

Opportunity is not distributed equally throughout society. For young people, the more privileged you are, the more likely you are to go to a top school, have access to additional educational opportunities outside of formal education, and be able to utilise your networks and resources to fuel your aspirations and aid your progress towards a fulfilling career. Those from more privileged backgrounds often have the wind beneath their wings in that they have greater means to gain the skills, competencies and critical information that empower people to thrive throughout their lives. Opportunity is not distributed equally throughout society; but things needn't be this way. Technology can and will redistribute opportunity, not by taking directly from the rich and giving to the poor, but by increasing the absolute supply and ensuring opportunities cannot be monopolised by elites. As I have already asserted, technology will enhance the effectiveness of educational institutions, it will disrupt and democratise the private tuition market, and it will equalise people's ambitions as it overcomes the siloed nature of people's lives. And this only scratches the surface of what technology can achieve. To be clear, this is not to say that technology is a panacea. I am not of the opinion that the onward march of innovation has the potential to put right all that is wrong with society. And more to the point, I am well aware that advanced technologies are not the solution to all the problems that give rise to social immobility. But technologies do have a critical role to play in equalising opportunity.

In Chapters 3 through to 7 I will delineate exactly where, why and how technologies can be utilised to level the playing field. In this chapter, however, I want to look under the bonnet and examine why, at a fundamental level, technology has the potential to enable a fairer distribution of opportunity. This chapter makes the case for technology by demonstrating how much more we can achieve with technology than without it. Moreover, in this chapter I'll argue that just as the features of a particular key make it the right solution for opening a particular lock, the aptitudes of technology will enable innovative solutions to unlock a wealth of opportunities for those who so often miss out. Here, I'm primarily concerned with what it is that technology has the capacity to do. A technology's fundamental aptitudes cannot be captured by describing how it is wired up or how it is programmed. Instead, these aptitudes should be understood by considering exactly how technologies extend human capabilities.

In concrete terms, the table below shows how certain aptitudes of technology align with a number of underlying problems that give rise to social immobility.

Technology can...	Automate and augment human labour	Capture, analyse and draw insight from data	Connect people and expand their horizons
This is good for social mobility because...	Products/services that aid people's developments will become more affordable and more readily available	Educators will be able to make better decisions, thereby enhancing their practice	Access to productive networks and formative experiences will become more equal
	Educational institutions will become more productive and therefore more effective	Institutions will be able to make fairer decisions at critical junctures	

Giving context to this table, a core problem that will need to be addressed if high levels of social mobility are to be realised is that opportunities often come with a hefty price tag. In Chapter 3 we'll explore the impact that private tuition has on social mobility, and in Chapter 7 we'll look at the impending importance of accessible provision for lifelong learning. The pertinent point here is that the high price of opportunities leads to there being a strong correlation between a person's financial means (or that of their family) and their access to services that develop their knowledge, skills and competencies – particularly in contexts where state-backed provision, subsidisation or loans are limited or non-existent. If some young people can't afford to benefit from private tuition but others can, then there are self-evident inequalities of opportunity. If developmental opportunities for adults to upskill and retrain become prerequisite for a fulfilling career but considerable means are required to access the best provision, then disparities in people's life chances will grow wider still.

Social mobility is also held back by the fact that educational institutions do not operate as productively as they could (by no fault of their own, I might add). Burdensome workloads divert the time and energies of educators away from more impactful tasks, which means that learners are not being optimally supported.[1] In Chapter 4, I'll explore this problem in the context of educational standards in schools. In particular, I'll show that people from less affluent backgrounds have the most to gain from this problem being combatted.

As well as being burdened by workload, educators are currently not in a position to fully exploit one of the most powerful resources for effective teaching and learning: information on their students' needs. This is perhaps better framed as an opportunity than a problem. In Chapter 4, I will detail how technology can help us seize this opportunity by empowering teachers (and learners themselves) with invaluable information. I'll also explain why this has the potential to raise educational standards significantly – again, especially for those from less affluent backgrounds.

Inability to extract a wealth of insights from the available information also hinders social mobility in another key respect. In numerous cases the ways in which aptitude is measured overlooks the genuine potential of many talented people. As I will show in Chapter 5 and again in Chapter 6, there is hence a tendency for the lights of the less privileged to remain hidden under a bushel.

Finally, disparities in people's networks, connections, and access to critical information and formative experiences also give rise to inequalities of opportunity.[2] In practice, this means that a person's ability to navigate the education system and the job market is correlated with their socioeconomic circumstances. Chapter 5 explores this problem in depth.

Each of these underlying problems can be addressed by utilising some combination of the fundamental aptitudes of technology outlined in the table above. Technologies can automate and augment human labour, which can increase the effectiveness and productivity of institutions and can enable products/services to become both more readily available and more affordable. As I will show, this will lead to significantly more affordable access to educational opportunities[3] (particularly those that are not typically free at the point of use). And it will also result in better performing educational institutions – a boon for social mobility as it tends to be the least privileged who are locked out of the best performing schools and colleges.

Technologies can capture, analyse, and draw insight from data at a scale that is not humanly possible. This allows humans to make better decisions, based on better information. As a result, the efficacy of educational institutions will be enhanced further still as teachers are empowered with far deeper insights into their learners' needs.[4] This capacity of technology will also enable fairer, more equitable decisions to be made at critical junctures, such as during admissions and recruitment processes.[5] Better contextual recruitment, for instance, will help employers find genuine talent that might otherwise have been overlooked. We'll revisit this point in Chapter 5.

Technologies can also connect us to experiences and to people typically outside our proximity. This can help us to forge fruitful new relationships and to expand our horizons. Being well connected and having access to opportunities are intrinsically linked. Case in point: in 1974, an influential study led by Mark Granovetter demonstrated that those who utilised their connections for employment purposes tended to secure better-paying jobs.[6] Without technologies, people's networks can be more limited, which advantages those who would naturally be connected to more 'useful' contacts (i.e., those who are better placed to support them effectively throughout their lives). But technology can democratise the development of productive networks. As the Pew Research Centre has noted, 'The internet helps build social capital'.[7]

Those who typically possess the least social capital evidently have the most to gain. As we will see, social media-style resources can help these people to build networks that rival those held by their more privileged peers.[8] And we should not be perturbed by the fact that ties developed via social media may be less intimate than ties established in person. Indeed, Granovetter demonstrated that weak ties can be 'indispensable to individuals' opportunities',[9] as they allow people to transcend their immediate circles and unlock new information and opportunities. He even showed that job opportunities were more likely to be sourced through weak ties than strong ties.

Equality of connectedness will help drive equality of opportunity. Fundamentally this is because being well connected improves the flow of critical information,[10] allowing the beneficiaries to make better decisions on how to develop themselves and improve their circumstances. Experiential technologies such as virtual reality, augmented reality and mixed reality will also help in this regard as users will be able to gain information directly from experiences they might not have otherwise have had access to. In Chapter 5, we'll explore how such technologies could be utilised in this respect to transform careers education.

All of the applications of technology that we will explore throughout this book have their roots in one or more of these three fundamental aptitudes. As will become, it is thanks to these very aptitudes that technologies have the ability to sever the link between a person's socioeconomic background and their life chances. Presently, we will explore the transformative power of these aptitudes by considering other domains in which they are already being harnessed to improve lives and make the world a better place. In doing so, I intend to whet your appetites for how the fundamental aptitudes of technologies can be harnessed to upgrade social mobility. I also aim to introduce you to a number of the technologies we'll explore throughout this book.

The fundamental aptitudes in action

Automation and augmentation

Before the printing press' powers of productivity made their mark on society, the production of books was a cumbersome, labour-intensive process in which they were written by hand. This resulted in books being a) in short supply and b) expensive, meaning that ownership of books, and therefore literacy itself, was often dominated by the rich and the powerful. But thanks to the inventiveness of Johannes Gutenberg, this unjust settlement did not last forever.[11]

Gutenberg's printing press, developed in the 1440s, meteorically scaled up production, causing prices to plummet as books became more and more plentiful. This had phenomenal consequences for society. The invention of the printing press has been credited with playing a role in facilitating the Reformation, the Renaissance and the Scientific Revolution.[12] The printing press is also acknowledged to have had a transformative impact on learning and education.[13] In *The Fourth Education Revolution,* Sir Anthony Seldon explains that the printing press precipitated the third education revolution, after which education became available to the masses. The fourth revolution, he argues, is being precipitated by artificial intelligence; we'll revisit this point later.

While there are debates over the precise role that the printing press played in the tectonic shifts that followed its invention, the significance of the mass production of books cannot be disputed.[14] One fundamental aptitude was prerequisite for the impact that the printing press had: automation. Alone, human scribes could only produce a fraction of the number of books that could be produced using a mechanised printing press. Without automation, books were scarce and expensive; with automation they became abundant and affordable. While automation is not invariably a force for good – a point I will address in Chapter 7 – the case of the printing press shows that this fundamental aptitude of technology can yield profoundly progressive outcomes. In particular, this example demonstrates that automation can disrupt elitist strongholds over ideas, knowledge and learning. A key lesson to learn is that if you want to challenge the hegemony of the elites, driving down costs is a good place to start.

It could be argued that the printing press is itself a historical example of how technologies can upgrade social mobility. After all, it was not the elites who primarily benefited from the resultant affordability of books. That said, the printing press is unlikely to play a role in improving upon current levels of social mobility. The fruits from that tree have already been picked. We hence need to turn our attention to contemporary innovations to understand where and how automating and augmentative technologies can level the playing field. Foremost among these innovations is artificial intelligence.

The UK government gives the following definition of artificial intelligence (AI):

> AI can be defined as the use of digital technology to create systems capable of performing tasks commonly thought to require intelligence.[15]

In order to develop a working knowledge of what AI is and how it can be utilised, it is important to familiarise oneself with the different types of AI and how they relate to each other.

For some, the term 'artificial intelligence' may conjure up images of machines that can rival human intelligence in all its glory. But in reality, AI is both more subtle and more intriguing. In *The 'no nonsense' guide to artificial intelligence*,[16] Priya Lakhani and Professor Rose Luckin (both visionary authorities in the applications of AI in education) note that, in order to understand the term 'artificial intelligence', it is helpful to start by making the distinction between two broad categories of AI. The first, General AI, is the term used to describe machines with comprehensive human-level intelligence. Echoing Lakhani and Luckin's elucidation, popular culture is brimming with examples of what General AI might look like (think of the films *2001: A Space Odyssey*, *Star Wars*, *Terminator*, and, of course, *A.I. Artificial Intelligence*).[17] But despite being a concept so firmly imprinted in our minds, General AI doesn't actually exist yet[18] – and there is no clear consensus on when (or if) AI will become so advanced. General AI may never exist; it may be years, decades or centuries from being achieved; or – the more worrying possibility – it may be just around the corner.[19] Regardless, this book does not speculate about the applications of General AI. Narrow AI on the other hand has already made its mark on the world.

Narrow AI systems have demonstrated their prowess by rivalling (and even surpassing) humans at well-defined tasks that generally require extraordinary levels of skill, and/or tactical and strategic brilliance. To expand on four of the examples of Narrow AI that Lakhani and Luckin provide, in 1997 IBM's Deep Blue beat world champion Garry Kasparov overall in a six-game chess match (in 1996 Deep Blue had beaten Kasparov in two individual games, but lost the match 4-2 overall).[20] Then, in 2016, DeepMind's AlphaGo programme beat Go champion Lee Sedol. Elsewhere, AI systems are also being applied to perform tasks that require humans to exhibit carefully honed intuition and well-trained judgement. In 2004, the USA's Defence Advanced Research Projects Agency (DARPA) held a Grand Challenge in which autonomous vehicles had to drive between Barstow, California, and Primm, Nevada. Fifteen vehicles entered the final round of the challenge with the hope of claiming the $1 million prize for the first vehicle across the finishing line, but none prevailed. When the Grand Challenge was held again in 2005, however, five autonomous vehicles succeeded in traversing 132 miles across the desert independently.[21] Self-driving cars may not be in mainstream use yet, but things may be heading in that direction. The technologies behind these vehicles are instances of Narrow AI because they exhibit human intelligence in order to serve their narrow, well-defined purpose – self-driving cars must emulate the judgement, knowledge and skill of human drivers in order to get from A to B safely.

AI systems have also shown the potential to master more creative thinking skills. In 2011, IBM's Watson triumphed against two former winners of the TV show *Jeopardy*. While chess requires astute logical thinking, *Jeopardy* requires the application of more lateral thinking skills.[22] Watson's victory was hence a clear demonstration of not only the depth, but also the breadth of intelligences that AI could exhibit. Looking towards the subcategories of General AI, it is important to recognise that the above examples are being grouped together under the umbrella of AI not because these systems all operate in the same way, but because they all achieve the goal of exhibiting human-level intelligence for a limited (but impressive) range of tasks. In actual fact, there are very clear dividing lines in terms of how AI systems function and why they are able to achieve their goals.

One branch of narrow AI is that of rules-based AI. Within this branch, system outputs (decisions, actions, etc.) are determined by the input from a user and a set of explicitly coded rules that software designers have written.[23] In educational contexts, one potential use of such systems could be to improve learners' creative writing. Given a picture of a haunted house, a learner could write a paragraph about how someone might feel if they entered said house. Here the primary input into the system is what the learner writes. The system may have been coded with rules that allow it to count the number of descriptive words a learner has used and identify whether they are using common or more ambitious lexical choices. The system's rules may also allow it to evaluate the use of spelling, punctuation and grammar. After these inputs have been processed in accordance with a set of pre-programmed rules, the output might be for the system to give the user feedback, such as:

> Well done, you have used a range of descriptive words (we've highlighted the adverbs you've used well in yellow, and the adjectives in orange) and your spelling, punctuation and grammar is spot on. To improve further still, you mind want to broaden your vocabulary. For instance, where you have written 'spooky' you could have used the word 'chilling' or 'ghastly.'

Rules-based systems can be particularly effective in cases where it is relatively straightforward to write a set of rules

– which should be obvious, really. But sometimes it is not so easy to write a set of rules to determine a particular outcome. It might be relatively simple to code your own rules for determining whether a sentence uses alliteration. But writing a set of rules to determine whether a sentence was expressing irony could be prohibitively demanding. That's where machine learning comes in.

As Lakhani and Luckin explain, with machine learning, systems are able to perform particular tasks despite not being explicitly coded to do so. 'Instead, the program is "trained" using large quantities of data and basic algorithms are written to allow it to "learn" from this training to perform a specific task.'[24] To train a machine learning system to recognise a dog, for instance, the system would be fed lots of examples of images that were tagged as being dogs. The machine would learn for itself the cluster of properties that determined whether something was a dog or not. Once the system has been trained, when you input an untagged picture of a Great Dane, its output would be to identify the thing in the picture as being a 'dog'. How did the system reach this conclusion? It made its own rules, so to speak, based on thorough statistical analysis of a huge number of data points. This analysis allowed the system to identify meaningful patterns and relationships within the data, and in turn enabled it to distinguish dogs from things that are not dogs.[25]

The example above is an instance of supervised machine learning because the system has been explicitly 'taught' what a dog is through large data sets of images that have been labelled as dogs. Supervised machine learning might also be applied to distinguish between sentences that expressed irony and those that didn't, or even to grade essays.

A distinct branch of machine learning is that of unsupervised machine learning. With this branch, systems are capable of clustering data together and drawing out meaningful patterns in datasets,[26] which allows people to make sense of seemingly erratic sprawls of information.[27] Unsupervised machine learning is used, for instance, to detect fraudulent banking activities.[28]

Reinforcement machine learning is a third branch. Here, systems are able to learn from their own performance and therefore continuously improve over time. Reinforcement machine learning can be used to enable computer programmes to play games. The programmes are effectively incentivised to get better at playing a game through a combination of 'trial and error' and 'carrot and stick'. If the programme plays well it is rewarded, and so it performs in that way more often; if it performs badly it is penalised, and so steers away from the behaviours that yielded these less favourable results.[29] AlphaGo was able to master the highly complex game of Go, thanks, in part, to reinforcement learning techniques.[30] The total number of moves that could possibly be made in a game of Go is greater than the number of particles in the universe. Due to the overwhelming number of move permutations, manually coding rules to determine the best move in any given situation is prohibitively difficult.[31] Machine learning techniques, however, are on much firmer ground.

By utilising AI (from rules-based AI to machine learning) humans can achieve more than they would otherwise be able to. A McKinsey Global Institute report entitled *Notes From The AI Frontier: Applying AI for Social Good*, presents a number of ways in which AI's capabilities could be used for social good. These include automatically detecting and removing hate speech online, identifying fires from satellite images, supporting wildlife conservation efforts and increasing accessibility for people with disabilities.

Let's take a closer look at the last two examples. Due to the tremendous complexity of the earth's ecosystems, conservation is a highly laborious endeavour. Conservationists need as much information as possible on the contexts in which they are working in order to protect wildlife and safeguard natural habitats. And they are often working against the clock as they parry external threats such as poaching and deforestation.[32] This means that there is a lot of work that needs to be done quickly. AI can be instrumental in lightening the load.

A 2011 study investigating the frequency with which birds collided with power cables on a Hawaiian island generated around 600 hours of audio recordings. To reach conclusions from their investigation, the researchers needed to identify how many times a collision could be heard. But wading through this volume of raw material is cumbersome and an inefficient use of a highly skilled researcher's time (note the parallels with workload burdens faced by teachers). For that reason, as Roberta Kwok, writing in an article published in the journal *Nature*, explains, the researchers enlisted the support of Conservation Metrics, whose AI software was able to automate the task of counting the frequency of collisions. This provided the researchers with critical information on the impact that power cables were having on populations of birds: information that enabled them to explore and advocate for interventions, such as installing flashing lights on power cables in order to deter birds from flying nearby.[33] By using AI to augment the work of human conservationists, this research team achieved greater productivity and efficiency.

The ability to get a lot of work done effectively and at pace is particularly important in time – sensitive contexts. It is therefore also fortunate that AI can be used to identify poachers in images and alert the relevant authorities.[34] Here AI resources are serving as additional pairs of eyes and ears, which endows conservationists with the 'manpower' needed to identify and address problems with urgency.[35]

While the boundary between automation and augmentation is not always clear-cut, in the cases described above it would be reasonable to classify AI as playing an augmentative role.

This is primarily because the AI systems are completing a contained sub-set of tasks and then handing responsibility for achieving the end goal (some form of action/strategy to protect wildlife) back to a person. In cases where AI can be used to support people with disabilities, however, AI is serving as more of an automator than an augmentor, because greater responsibility is being placed on it to achieve the end goal by itself.

Automation facilitates independence. YouTube, for instance, uses speech-to-text software to automatically caption videos. This enables deaf users to access and enjoy content without having to depend on other people.[36] Ava, a mobile app that has helped over 100,000 users, supports group conversations by translating speech into text, almost in real time, so that deaf people can be included in the discussion.[37] Technologies are also emerging that could translate sign language.[38] To be clear, this is not to say that AI-based accessibility will address all challenges faced by the deaf community. But there is no doubt that these innovations will bring significant benefits to those who are so often excluded.

While there are justifiable concerns that AI's ability to augment and automate could displace human labour and lead to higher levels of unemployment (concerns that I share), the above examples show that these propensities of AI are equally capable of great good. By performing tasks that would usually require human intelligence, AI can amplify the impacts of humans acting alone. As I will show in the upcoming chapters, just as AI can be used to enhance conservation efforts and provide direct support to marginalised groups, AI can also be used to boost the efficacy of educational institutions and provide educational opportunities where there were previously none.

When discussing automation and augmentation in the context of education, however, a point that needs to be reiterated is that we are dealing with Narrow AI and not

General AI. For the foreseeable future, AI will be too limited in its capabilities to act as a substitute for an expert human teacher.[39] Personally, I am of the opinion that it will never reach this point. But as we will see, AI can perform many tasks that other technologies cannot: from marking students' work all the way up to providing tailored support that can rival the efficacy of many commonplace methods of teaching and learning. As I will argue, AI may even be able to surpass the efficacy of one-to-one tutoring from a non-expert (note, though, that this takes into account quantity of provision, not just quality). That said, we should not be under any illusion that AI is a match for an outstanding, inspiring teacher. In contexts where teachers are readily available, AI should be used to augment teachers' practice and free up their time by automating the tasks that divert teachers' energies away from supporting learners directly.[40] In contexts where teachers are not readily available, AI's most advanced capabilities should be utilised to give learners the next best thing. This principle applies as much to the private tuition market, which many people have limited access to, as it does to the case of school closures during lockdown, where the vast majority of learners had limited access to teachers.

Extracting insights from data

Looking through the lens of automation and augmentation alone does not provide a full view of what technology can achieve and why. For a start, we also need to consider that one of technology's most transformative capacities is its ability to capture, analyse and gain insight from data in a way that is not humanly possible.

'The world's most valuable resource is no longer oil, but data', asserted *The Economist* as part of a 2017 leader article.[41] The value of data lies in the fact that better data leads to better information, which enables improved decision making and hence more effective actions. As a result, the increased utilisation of data is transforming industries and reshaping the world around us. Many retail giants, for instance, are using data insights to better target their products at consumers,[42] manufacturers are using advanced analytics to improve product yields,[43] and data insights can even be used to reduce cities' carbon footprints. Data from embedded sensors in street lighting enables the city of Copenhagen to minimise the amount of energy used to light its streets, for instance.[44]

The use of data to support decision making is not new, but due to advances in technology there has been a step change in the level of insight that can be drawn from this precious resource. We have now moved into the age of big data, which is characterised by the volume of data collected, the velocity at which it is captured and processed, and the variety of data that can be made use of.[45] Big data and artificial intelligence are distinct but related concepts. Big data, as the name implies, refers to the data itself. The colossal amount of data involved means that insights cannot be extracted from big data using conventional methods of data analysis.[46] Instead, sophisticated techniques are required to convert big data into 'big information', and machine learning is often used as part of this process. Reciprocally, big data can be instrumental in the development of machine learning systems as it provides the enormous amounts of data needed to train these systems.[47]

The ability to extract rich insights from large volumes of data can lead to a plethora of societal benefits. A pertinent example that stands out at the time of writing is that of the insights gained from data fed into the Covid Symptom Tracker app. Over 4 million people used the app to record any symptoms they were exhibiting at any particular time. Collectively, from the data amassed, researchers were able to conclude that a loss of taste and smell was the most predictive symptom of coronavirus. Researchers were also able to draw conclusions on how vulnerability to the virus varied based on certain underlying health conditions.[48] The wealth of information gleaned from the Covid Symptom Tracker's data sets made healthcare systems and society as a whole better placed to protect the most vulnerable, and better equipped to monitor and hence mitigate the spread of the virus. It has even been argued that big data could enable the economic impacts of the pandemic to be more closely monitored,[49] which could allow for better informed responses from governments.

Elsewhere, data insights have been used to support areas afflicted by droughts by efficiently targeting the distribution of water tankers. Moulton Niguel Water District in California, for instance, saved $25 million by using data analytics to predict demand for water at a granular level.[50]

The underlying principle here is simple: when grappling with issues that can have a significant impact on people's lives, having as much useful information as possible pays dividends. This principle is already being put into practice in education as part of the emerging practice of learning analytics. As noted in the Higher Education Commission's report, *From Bricks to Clicks*, as students digitally interact with their universities, they create a 'data footprint', which universities can use to 'optimise the student experience'.[51] As Jisc has explained, this footprint can be built up when students take actions such as 'going to the library, logging into their virtual learning environment or submitting assessments online'.[52] By distilling key information from students' digital footprints, universities are able to achieve positive outcomes for students. The University of New England, for instance, cut drop-out rates by a third by utilising data insights effectively.[53]

Promisingly, learning analytics is also being leveraged to address achievement gaps between different groups of learners. Both the University of Derby and Nottingham Trent University are pioneering this practice. The former has used learning analytics to provide evidence-based support for BME students; the latter has used insights to inform individualised approaches to supporting at-risk students.[54]

While learning analytics has often been used at a macroscopic level, allowing institutions to intervene at critical junctures, the principles it instantiates can also be applied to improve teaching and learning on an ongoing basis. As I will discuss in depth in Chapter 4, educators already feed off information (as do learners themselves). Understanding an individual learner's needs is the key to effective teaching. Data analytics and education are therefore a match made in heaven. As we'll see, data-driven technologies are primed to have as transformative an impact in education as they are having in other industries. Technology's capacity to automate and augment will enable educators to focus more of their time on high-impact tasks; in parallel, technology's capacity to draw insight from data will enable educators to be even more impactful than they would otherwise have been.[55] This is phenomenally good news for all learners, particularly those who typically miss out on the highest standards of teaching.

Extracting insights from data plus automation and augmentation

As well as operating in parallel, the fundamental aptitudes of automation and augmentation, and of being able to extract insights from data can also be deployed in tandem. In many cases a technological system will first mine for insights, and will then automatically take action based on such insights. Smart Agriculture provides an example of how these aptitudes work together to achieve vitally important outcomes.

From the capturing of data all the way up to taking action automatically, Smart Agriculture systems play a key role in the effective and efficient functioning of farms.[56] Given that the world's population (and therefore demand for food) is growing, arable land is becoming increasingly scarce, and climate change is creating unprecedented challenges for the agriculture industry,[57] innovations such as Smart Agriculture are desperately needed to sustain human life on earth. Fundamentally, such systems enable better decisions to be made about how to utilise precious resources, and they ensure that the necessary actions are taken in a timely and accurate manner.

Smart Agriculture in effect customises the operations of a particular farm based on its fluctuating features and conditions. If the weather changes, for instance, the system would change responsively. Ongoing customisation of systems to particular contexts (or users) is not only seen in macroscopic systems such as Smart Agriculture. There is a wide family of adaptive and responsive systems that can be understood as cases where technologies combine the two key aptitudes of automation and augmentation, and of being able to extract insight from data.

Intelligent Tutoring Systems and adaptive learning platforms (technologies we'll explore in Chapters 3 and 4) are among the most pertinent examples for the social mobility cause. Because these adaptive, responsive systems are capable of enhanced decision-making and automated action, they are particularly proficient at providing high-quality provision at scale. These resources are already having a positive impact on learning and their effectiveness will only increase. Just as the printing press disrupted the elite's stranglehold on knowledge and ideas, advanced educational technologies will democratise access to a significant proportion of the learning and development opportunities available outside of formal education.

Note that, as well as being able to take end-to-end responsibility for supporting an individual's learning, these innovations can also be used in a way that hands back responsibility to teachers for addressing the needs of learners: those which have been identified through the platform. Just because a technological system can take automated action, does not mean it always should or that it inevitably will. Indeed, as we will see throughout the book, even the most advanced technologies can be used alongside human experts symbiotically.

Connection

By connecting people to each other and to otherwise inaccessible experiences, technologies can render people less constrained by their immediate circumstances. The example of online dating demonstrates that technology's ability to connect people to each other can have life-changing consequences. Online dating platforms provide new opportunities for people to meet, thereby increasing the number of people one could potentially enter into a relationship with. Many people have benefited from these platforms. A survey by the Pew Research Center found that 12% of Americans have either married or had a 'committed relationship' with a person they met via an online dating platform.[58] Michael Rosenfeld, a sociology professor at Stanford University, has argued that these technologies have been particularly beneficial to those who previously would have had limited opportunities to meet new people.[59]

Elsewhere, academics Philipp Hergovich and Josue Ortega have developed statistical models that suggest that online dating apps are spurring integration among people from different ethnicities through increased interracial marriage. In their own words: 'Social integration occurs rapidly when a society benefits from new connections'.[60]

I would argue that tools that make it easier for a person to meet the love of their life are even more life-changing than tools that expand people's professional networks. But the important point here is the parallel between the two cases.

Without the support of online dating apps, some people will find they have few opportunities to make new acquaintances and meet potential suitors. For many, colleagues are off limits and friends of friends is an ever-diminishing pool. In other cases, a person's sexuality may result in their being fewer options.[61] Dating apps therefore render people less siloed. With professional networking tools, the exact same principles apply. Imagine that you are thirteen years old and you want to be a lawyer. You have pounded the search engines to find out as much information as possible, and you now have a pretty good idea of what the job entails and how to get there. But your hard-earned knowledge is likely to pale in comparison to actually knowing a lawyer who can give you tangible unfiltered insights into how to get in and how to get on.[62]

In this sense, people who have more limited professional networks face similar issues to people who know few potential companions. The salient difference is that in one case increased connectivity is a means to an end (getting a good job), and in the other it is an end in itself (meeting a potential partner). But the crucial likeness is that both issues can be addressed by increasing the network of people that one is connected to. In Chapters 5 and 6 I'll demonstrate how social media-style technologies could be used to empower young people with fruitful networks while they are at the foothills of their journey towards a fulfilling working life. For the cause of social mobility, it is particularly important that young people from all backgrounds can be connected to a wide variety of professionals so that they can get direct insights to inform their career trajectories. To allow for a long run-up, starting early is key. Of course, this does create its own set of challenges, but these challenges are surmountable. Robust safeguarding protocols will need to be put in place; and perhaps parents, schools or both may need to actively oversee young people's use of such platforms.

Another set of challenges arises from the risk that connections made via such platforms could be of a more transient nature than relationships formed in person. While I have already addressed the point that weak ties have been shown to be more valuable for professional networking than strong ties, there is still the question of whether an over-reliance on technology could pose opportunity costs if schools, colleges and universities come to eschew more personal means of expanding one's networks and experiences. As I will show in Chapters 5 and 6, this set of challenges is equally surmountable. The key is to take a multi-pronged approach. Social media-style tools should be used to increase the breadth of useful connections that people have access to, and in-person interactions should be used to deepen the impact that new-found connections can have on one's life chances.

This rule of thumb can also be applied when using experiential technologies to broaden young people's horizons. As I will show, technologies such as virtual reality (VR) can be used to make people feel more connected to experiences and lifestyles that might otherwise have been alien to them. We'll explore how this aptitude can be mobilised to enhance careers guidance, but let's first consider where else it is making a difference.

Telling most people about the suffering of refugees fleeing war-torn countries is likely to elicit some sympathy; but actually showing them the harshness of these people's lives is more likely to spur them to take action. When it comes to giving people a tangible – in this case, visceral – sense of what it's like 'to be in someone else's shoes',[63] VR has much to offer. UNICEF has harnessed this innovation to show people what life is like for Sidra, a 12-year-old girl living in Zaatari Refugee Camp alongside approximately 80,000 people who have fled Syria.[64] Elsewhere, researchers at Stanford University have shown that immersing people in a VR experience on homelessness is more effective at persuading people to sign a petition on affordable housing than passive forms of communication that cover the same content.[65] As

PwC commented, 'VR doesn't just encourage empathy, it transforms empathetic feeling into altruistic action.'[66]

The pertinent point here for the context of social mobility is that immersive technologies allow you to really experience and be impacted by new contexts in ways that other technologies don't. Think of how much more our thirteen-year-old aspiring lawyer would get out of a virtual courtroom experience compared to reading an overview of what to expect in court. Experiential technologies will be instrumental in expanding people's horizons and solidifying people's aspirations.

In summary

The first purpose of the above discussion was to whet your appetite for what can be achieved when we purposefully apply technologies to solve a particular problem or to seize a specific opportunity. The second was to explain exactly why it is that we can achieve more with technology than without. By virtue of the three fundamental aptitudes that we have explored, technology has proven its mettle by supporting people to address headline challenges, from sustainability to the Covid-19 pandemic. And while the examples we have explored above are all fantastically beneficial applications of technology, this book is not about how technology can be used to confront global warming, manage infectious diseases or protect endangered species. But as we will see, and as I have indicated throughout this chapter, the very same aptitudes of technology can and will play a significant role in equalising opportunity and therefore boosting social mobility.

Those who are not from privileged backgrounds stand to gain the most from the impending surge in supply of opportunity. That said, the advantages will be felt universally; everyone stands to benefit. Take the prosaic capacity of technology to connect people to others who are not in the same room as them. Without technology's ability to facilitate these interactions over a distance, students at schools and universities around the world may not have had any direct interaction with their teachers/lecturers during lockdown.

Next consider that at the time of writing, the pressures on teachers and schools have gone through the roof. By enabling educators to focus on teaching learners effectively and safely, technologies capable of automating tasks could help to buttress the effectiveness of schools during these difficult times – something that is very much in the interests of all members of society.

Furthermore, the most advanced educational technologies could be indispensable for securing a strong baseline of learning for everyone. AI resources are able to structure and advance people's developments with outstanding effectiveness. If schools do close their doors again, these resources cannot be left on the shelf.

Technology is not merely a wartime consigliere, however. The aptitudes of technology will also yield increased opportunities for all as societies move into the new normal. Just because someone's godmother is a City lawyer does not mean they necessarily have access to networks that will support their progress towards becoming a UX designer. And just because someone's parents are wealthy does not mean they do not have complex educational needs that could be better met via enhanced insights into them as a learner. Tools that evaluate learners' needs effectively will improve provision for people from all socioeconomic backgrounds.

One final point to stress is that technology is not going to solve all of the problems that give rise to social immobility. I have enumerated the ways in which the aptitudes of technology can be used to break many of the shackles binding a person's life chances to their socioeconomic background. But the list of shackles I have enumerated is not exhaustive, and there are limitations to what technology can achieve. In Chapter 9

I will confront the issues that cannot readily be addressed by technology. But do not be disheartened. There are ways to solve problems other than by utilising technology. That said, as we will see in the following chapters, technology itself will allow us to make remarkable strides towards a more socially mobile society.

CHAPTER 3

DISRUPTING THE SHADOW
EDUCATION SYSTEM

As I have already noted, parents and guardians want the best for their children. This is not only natural, it is a good thing. And it is also a good thing that parents work hard to provide the best for their children, which includes doing their utmost to support their child's educational development. It really should be no surprise, therefore, that many parents decide to pay for private tuition, a service that allows its beneficiaries to catch up, grow in confidence, feel prepared for upcoming assessments or entrance exams, and experience a host of other advantages.[1] What should be equally unsurprising is that private tuition, a relatively expensive, labour-intensive service, is not equally accessed by all groups of people; its rewards are not spread evenly throughout society, and as a result private tuition is a driver of social immobility.

Shadow Schooling: Private Tuition and Social Mobility in the UK, a report from the Sutton Trust that explores the shadow education system that has emerged due to widespread uptake of private tuition, demonstrates that children from more advantaged families are nearly 50% more likely to have received private tuition than those from the least well-off families (those who are eligible for free school meals). The report also showed that children who attend private schools are twice as likely to benefit from private tuition as children who attend state schools; and that, when polled, over a third of those who did not participate in private tuition cited the high cost as a reason why.[2]

According to the aforementioned report, private tuition costs around £24 per hour (rising to around £27 in London), with one hour of tuition a week for five to six months being the norm. Taking these figures together, a rough estimate of the minimum cost for a sustained period of private tuition would be £520. Then take into account that many families have more than one child of school age, and it becomes clear that access to private tuition is highly dependent on a family's disposable income.

As demonstrated by polling from the Sutton Trust, the most common reasons why tutees access private tutoring are to gain general help with their schoolwork, to help them do well in specific exams and to help them with a school entrance test.[3] Elsewhere, there is compelling evidence that private tuition in the form of coaching has a significant impact on children's chances of passing the 11+ and therefore going on to attend grammar schools. Statistics from the FFT Education Datalab show that among children living in areas with grammar schools, 73% of pupils who were coached for the 11+ passed and went on to attend grammar school, whereas only 14% of children who were not coached achieved this outcome.[4] It has also been demonstrated that parents in the top income bracket are 'three to four times more likely to have used a private tutor to help their child get into grammar school' than parents with lower incomes.[5] These facts combined go some way to explaining why less than 3% of pupils who attend grammar schools are eligible for free school meals, even though 18% of all pupils in areas with selective education are eligible.[6] There are also indications that students are being tutored to prepare them for university admissions tests, including those for Oxbridge.[7]

For those who have access to it, private tuition provides an opportunity for valuable educational development over and above the opportunities provided by formal education. This opportunity translates to concrete benefits, which range from feeling more confident in one's writing ability after some intensive one-to-one support, all the way to doing better in one's GCSEs or other formal exams, which in turn may open the door to additional pathways in the future. But as this channel of opportunity is disproportionately accessed by more affluent young people, the benefits of private tuition are not distributed equally throughout society. Our attention must hence turn to finding a means of extending the benefits of private tuition to everyone.

At first glance, the solution seems obvious. Surely, we just need to ensure that all learners can access private tuition. The current problematic situation is that some learners benefit from individualised support from a private tutor but others don't; it stands to reason that the ideal situation is for all people to benefit from this same service. This is almost certainly correct. The ideal solution would be to enable universal access to one-to-one tuition from a private tutor. But as I will show, any achievable version of this ideal would still struggle to equalise opportunity within the shadow education system. An innovative solution is needed to equalise access to the benefits that are currently achieved through private tuition. Intelligent Tutoring Systems (ITSs) are the best candidates.[8]

The authoritative report, *Intelligence Unleashed: An Argument for AI in Education* cogently makes the case that ITSs could enable every single learner to benefit from 'an intelligent, personal tutor'. The report explains that ITSs utilise artificial intelligence to 'simulate one-to-one human tutoring' by tailoring learning activities to individual learners' needs, and by supporting learners with feedback, as and when it is needed.[9] As discussed in *Intelligence Unleashed*, the learning activities mentioned above could include videos, games or even VR-based experiences. Just like a human tutor, an ITS might be able to judge what difficulty level each task should be set at and what type of activity each student would respond best to. And if a learner needed support with a particular question, problem or activity, the ITS may well be able to provide it. For instance, Aida, an app created by Pearson, which provides adaptive support with calculus, can analyse students' working out 'line by line'.[10] This allows for pinpointed feedback and support, and enables students to be '[guided] through the solution'.[11]

ITSs have the potential to disrupt the shadow education system. They are affordable, they can be accessed at whatever time and for however long a learner wishes, and they can deliver high-quality provision. Each of these factors are necessary ingredients for combatting social immobility. As asserted in Chapter 2, affordable resources/services ensure that certain channels of opportunity cannot be dominated by the more affluent and closed off to the underprivileged. In the case of ITSs, where higher usage will often confer greater benefits at no additional cost, the link between financial means and access to opportunity stands to be critically disrupted. But this is conditional on the efficacy of ITSs. A textbook or an online quiz site are both affordable and can be used as much as one pleases. However, these resources do not open up the benefits of private tuition universally, even if they do extend educational opportunities to some extent. ITSs represent a paradigm shift in the quality and efficacy of resources for learning outside of formal education. Indeed, ITSs may be of such high quality that attending sessions with a private tutor may no longer be necessary for achieving the benefits of private tuition. A 2016 meta-analysis published in the *Review of Education Research* even indicated that ITSs could 'match the success of human tutoring'.[12] The shadow education sector is being brought into the light.

The idea of computer software playing the role of a private tutor may make some feel a little squeamish. Arguing that mass access to high-performing ITSs will mean that private tuition can no longer monopolise opportunities within the shadow education system seems to imply that private tutors can be readily rivalled by machines. Some may deduce from this that humans have nothing special to add to the education equation and that the interpersonal aspects of learning are dispensable. But this deduction is invalid. Talented, inspirational human educators are absolutely vital: to be clear, technology will not replace teachers. That said, technology could rival the impacts achieved by private tutors, not because they are better at supporting learners than high performing tutors – although ITSs could be more effective than a poor or even mediocre tutor, as shown by the meta-analysis referred to above – but because optimal flexibility and inexhaustible availability have never been human strong suits, meaning that ITSs are well placed to excel in the context of on-demand and ongoing learning.

Although ITSs might never be the inspiring role models that the very best tutors are, they do closely emulate a cluster of key skills exhibited by human tutors. If you were going to hire a maths tutor to support yourself or a family member , you'd want to be confident that they actually knew their stuff (had relevant subject knowledge), that they understood how to teach mathematical concepts (had sufficient pedagogical skill) and that they were able to fine-tune their tutoring to each individual's needs. Effective ITSs are vested with all three of these capacities too. With some ITSs, these capacities are codified in the form of the domain model, the pedagogical model and the learner model, respectively. In other cases, ITSs use more flexible approaches, which tend to utilise machine learning.[13]

In order for ITSs to provide effective and engaging learning experiences, excellent learning material is key. Many EdTech companies use qualified teachers to ensure that their platform content is of the highest quality. Squirrel Ai – the creators of an innovative AI-powered adaptive learning system[14], which is used by more than two million students[15] – employs the services of many of China's recognised 'master teachers' to help develop curricula.[16]

ITSs are also designed with an understanding of how students learn. Designers need to know when feedback should be used, how and when systems should assess a learner's understanding and how misconceptions could be addressed. In essence, ITSs need to be able to build upon highly effective teaching practices.[17] ASSISTments, an ITS developed by Worcester Polytechnic Institute, for instance, makes use of adaptive feedback techniques such as 'hints' and 'scaffolding problems that provide worked examples' in order to support learners.[18]

Finally, ITSs are able to customise provision to the needs of individual learners. All learners are unique. People learn in different ways and how any individual learns best will vary depending on a host of factors including how they are feeling and even how hungry they are. Either via learner models or through alternative approaches, ITSs build up a picture of each individual learner in order to decide how best to support their own unique needs at any given time. The learner model will draw upon information from a learner's historical interactions with the platform to understand their strengths and needs in a holistic way. It may also use data inputs to infer details of their levels of engagement and/or emotional states.[19]

To get a sense of why this capability makes such a difference to the quality of intelligent tutoring, we can think about the qualities we would expect of human tutors. For instance, a mediocre tutor will at the very least need to be able to judge that because a tutee misidentified a cell wall as a cell membrane, they may need to recap the parts of a cell and then be assessed again to check that they have understood. A quite good tutor should be able to recognise that the tutee is not only struggling with differentiating between cell walls and cell membranes, but is also unable to identify vacuoles or define what a cell nucleus is, and hence hypothesise that they may not have a good understanding of the foundations of cell biology. Here, our quite good tutor is able to draw together different pieces of information to make more sophisticated judgements on the best way to support a particular learner. A really good tutor should go further still. They may be able to detect that the learner actually feels quite embarrassed about the fact they have not yet mastered a supposedly basic topic. The really good tutor may hence realise that motivating the learner is going to be just as important as providing them with well-designed learning activities to teach the topic. And if the tutor is really as good as they say they are, they may even be able to judge how best to motivate the learner, based on an evaluation of what strategies have worked well in the past and how similar the context they worked in is to the current situation. The really good tutor earns their title because they have a good conception of the learner's underlying needs, and because they understand the factors that support their learning.

Like the very best tutors, ITSs are designed to develop a rounded understanding of each learner based on a plethora of insights. Equipped with well-designed content, an understanding of how people learn and the ability to tailor learning to the needs of individual students, ITSs ensure that users can experience high-quality, adaptive learning – and as much of it as they wish. As we've seen, there are even indications that ITSs could rival the impacts of human tutoring, and at a fraction of the cost. I am hence firmly of the opinion that a universal uptake of ITSs is the best way to equalise opportunity within the shadow education system. My optimism aside, other approaches also deserve a fair hearing.

The analogue approach (and its challenges)

ITSs are not the only option that has been put forward to make the shadow education system more inclusive. In their 2016 report, *Shadow Schooling*, the Sutton Trust made a number of recommendations to equalise access to private tuition, including the introduction of a means-tested voucher scheme, the aim of which would be to allow lower-income families to directly access private tuition.

A means-tested voucher scheme would definitely go part of the way to resolving the inequalities of opportunity that private tuition gives rise to, but tech-based solutions can enable even greater progress towards equality of opportunity within the shadow education system.

A key factor is that tech-based solutions are inherently more scalable. With regards to delivering a voucher scheme, the first hurdles to overcome are the intertwined factors of the availability of tutors and the variation in performance between them.[20] A voucher scheme simply would not work if there weren't enough tutors to go around. And if a sufficient quantity of tutors were to enter the market to meet new demand, but at the expense of tutor quality, there would be a real risk that those who can afford to pay directly will access the best tutors, and that those who paid with vouchers would only have access to the poorest-performing tutors. Disparities in access to tuition may just be replaced with disparities in the quality of the tuition.

Let's work out what we're up against. At the beginning of 2019, 15.4% of pupils in UK schools were eligible for and claiming free school meals.[21] According to the *Shadow Schooling* report, in 2015 just 10% of all state-educated secondary school pupils received private tuition. So in order to ensure that all pupils who are eligible for free school meals have the option of receiving private tuition, the marketplace will have to expand considerably. If all eligible pupils used their vouchers, if they received tuition at a comparable rate to the 10% of secondary pupils who received tutoring in 2015, and if none of these pupils would have otherwise accessed tuition, then the marketplace for tutoring would need to increase by 154%. Even if we assume that some of these pupils would have otherwise received tuition, a total increase in the supply of tutoring of 100% could well be needed. This would mean either twice as many tutors, tutors working twice as much, or – more likely – some combination of the two.

It is difficult to give an exact figure for how many additional tutors would have to enter the market for this increase in supply to be satisfied. For one thing, there is insufficient data on the current stock of tutors to predict how much of this additional supply could be met by existing tutors working more hours. And more importantly, we don't even know how many people are currently working as tutors, so we can't readily calculate what a 100% increase in tutor numbers would be. By some estimates, the current market contains 1.5 million tutors, which would imply that another 1.5 million may be needed to ensure demand doesn't outstrip supply. As noted by the Sutton Trust, this figure is likely to be an overestimate.[22] But recruiting a mere tenth of this quantity could prove problematic considering that we must go to any length to ensure the quality of tutoring is not compromised.

Even if we do recruit enough high-quality tutors, with a voucher scheme it would be difficult to guard against those with the means to do so regaining their advantage by purchasing more hours of tuition. Yes, the law of diminishing returns will kick in eventually, but it seems likely that there would be significant benefits gained from receiving three or four hours of tuition a week, compared to one or two.

The most pressing concern of all, however, is that a voucher scheme won't necessarily distribute opportunity all that equally, as those who just miss out on pupil premium funding (or whatever proxy is used to allocate vouchers) will miss out on free tuition entirely. The whole point of a technology-driven solution, on the other hand, is to vanquish each of the impediments to equality of opportunity mentioned above. When ITSs become prevalent (which I hope they will) those with means will not be able to unfairly protect their advantage. They won't be able to just get a better ITS because all such systems will be affordable and of a consistently high standard. And all learners will have access to an endless amount of support, meaning families with more disposable income won't be able to just buy more hours of tutoring than those with less money to spare. This innovation genuinely has the potential to level the playing field.

To reassert, there is no suggestion here that ITSs are better than high-quality human tutors. If the human resources existed to provide every learner with a personal human tutor who was a) an exceptional educator, b) indefatigably available 24/7 and c) charging rates cheap enough so as to be affordable for every family, then that is the system we would go with. But it is not clear that any one of those criteria can be fulfilled, and it is perfectly clear that all of those criteria cannot be fulfilled together... or is it?

What about the National Tutoring Programme?

In June 2020, three months after UK schools closed in order to stem the spread of coronavirus, an exciting new project was announced, which made me question my logic. The National Tutoring Programme (NTP) was established to allow state schools to access a pool of excellent tutors, which would enable their most in-need students to get extra support.[23] Optimistic that the NTP would help to address the inequities exacerbated during the pandemic, I began to wonder whether I had been too quick to dismiss the merits of making human tutoring available en masse. Was this in fact the best way to bring balance to the shadow education system?

Like many others, I am hopeful that the NTP will successfully help to address attainment gaps, which are likely to have widened as a result of the pandemic.[24] That said, I am still concerned that unless our most powerful innovations are fully utilised, growing inequalities in the shadow education system could significantly undermine progress made by schools.

During school closures, demand for private tuition skyrocketed.[25] Given that many families are anxious about the long-term educational impacts of school closures, there is good reason to believe that this increased demand within the shadow education system could be sustained in the long term. For some families at least, greater spending on private tuition could become part of the new normal. But without efforts to equalise opportunities, this could be perilous for social mobility. Private tuition outside of school could go from being a beneficial boost for some, to becoming the dividing line between those who get ahead and those who are left behind. Even with the support of the NTP, without further increases in the resources available to them, schools may struggle to counteract the impacts of a flourishing but exclusive shadow education system.

This indicates a two-pronged approach. Firstly, we need to make schools so effective that the shadow education system can only yield ever-diminishing returns. If schools were optimally effective, there would be very little reason to seek additional provision elsewhere. Moreover, the formal education system could actually aim to subsume its shadowy twin entirely. In the next chapter, we will explore how the shadow education system can be illuminated and brought into the light.

Secondly, until we have reached the point where the shadow education system has been fully integrated into formal schooling, we must decisively equalise opportunities within it. Wealthy families will inevitably win the 'educational arms race'[26] until wealth ceases to confer any advantage. But as we have seen with the case of the printing press, driving down prices can critically weaken the dominance of the privileged. ITSs will increase the affordability and availability of high-quality developmental opportunities outside of the formal education sector, and hence make the benefits of private tuition available to all.

Not to detract from the credible and exciting prospect of an equalised, or perhaps even illuminated, shadow education system, I would like to end this chapter by acknowledging two caveats. First, a critical question hangs in the air. Even if the software itself is inexpensive, wouldn't there still be prohibitive inequalities in accessing ITSs if the necessary hardware was beyond the means of some families? The simple answer is yes... but this problem can be decisively overcome. I'll give this point the attention it deserves in Chapter 8.

Secondly, it should be recognised that private tuition is not the only channel of opportunity that aids people's developments outside of formal education. Research by the University of Bath and the Social Mobility Commission found that young people from lower-income households were significantly less likely to participate in extra-curricular activities such as arts and sports. The research also showed that participation in these activities increased young people's confidence, motivation and aspirations.[27] To address this asymmetry, the Commission advocated for a national bursary scheme, the aim of which would be to enable young people from disadvantaged backgrounds to access extra-curricular activities. Measures such as this will also be necessary if we are to truly equalise the shadow education system.

CHAPTER 4

EQUALITY OF EXCELLENCE (MAKING SCHOOLS ENGINES OF SOCIAL MOBILITY)

Our education system is not the 'engine of social mobility' that it could and should be.[1] This is poignantly demonstrated by the fact that when young people leave secondary school, the attainment gap between disadvantaged and non-disadvantaged students is equivalent to 1.5 years of schooling. For those young people suffering the most severe levels of destitution, the gap is closer to two years.[2] Yes, schools do inherit a pre-existing advantage gap, with the most disadvantaged young people starting school 4.3 months behind their peers,[3] but despite not being the cause of inequality of opportunity, schools must be supported to level the playing field to a greater extent. So what needs to change to enable our schools to become engines of social mobility?

To answer this question, we first need to acknowledge that the attainment gap specified above can be explained, to a significant extent, by the fact that disadvantaged children are far less likely to attend a high-performing school than their more advantaged peers, as shown by the following analysis from the Economic and Social Research Council:

The achievement advantage of children of higher educated parents relative to those of lower educated parents widens throughout the school years. This widening gap is almost entirely accounted for by the fact that children from degree-educated parents are far more likely to attend higher performing secondary schools and so benefit from a positive school effect.[4]

If the school system as a whole is to become an engine of social mobility, it is imperative that this injustice is put right.

Taking a closer look at the problem, across the comprehensive sector, 17.2% of pupils are eligible for free school meals (FSM), but only 9.4% of the pupils at England's top 500 comprehensive schools fall into this category.[5] This is strongly linked to the fact that good schools are often embedded in relatively wealthy communities. In England, 12.8% of pupils in the catchment area of the best schools are eligible for FSM (4.4 percentage points below the expected value) and in Scotland the figure is only 9.1%.[6] Research has even shown that a child from a poorer family is nine times more likely than a child from a wealthier family to attend a school that has been rated inadequate by Ofsted.[7] And this problem is dynamic too. Living within the catchment of one of the top 500 comprehensive schools can lead to a significant increase in house prices,[8] meaning that as schools improve, less affluent families are often 'priced out' of the catchment area and therefore less likely to attend these flourishing schools.[9]

As well as inequalities in access to good schools, pupils from different backgrounds also experience related inequalities in teaching standards. The following key findings from the All-Party Parliamentary Group on Social Mobility paint a bleak picture. A pupil from a disadvantaged background is 'more likely to be taught by teachers who are less experienced and have lower qualifications'.[10] The crisis in teacher retention and recruitment (more on this momentarily) is particularly acute in highly deprived areas and therefore affects disadvantaged pupils most severely.[11] And pupils in deprived areas are 22% less likely to be taught physics by a teacher with a related degree.[12]

Then there is the issue of gaming school admissions processes, whereby some parents bend the rules to give their children a higher chance of getting into the best schools – perhaps by renting or buying a home near a top school, which can be far too expensive an investment for less well-off families.[13]

We should not lose sight of the simple nature of the underlying problem, however, which can be summarised as follows:

1. Schools are not of a uniformly high standard, therefore some people inevitably go to better schools (and experience better teaching) than other people.

2. In our current system, disadvantaged pupils are disproportionately under-represented at the best schools and over-represented at the worst.

Moving forward, there are two flanks upon which to address educational inequality.

To counteract point 2, one could focus their attention on designing policies that ensure all socioeconomic groups are equally represented in the best and worst schools on offer.

Policy prescriptions in this category might include measures to counteract the gaming of school admissions systems,[14] increased incentives for schools to admit more disadvantaged pupils or quotas that compel schools to admit a proportionate number of disadvantaged pupils.

Social mobility-oriented policies often hail from this set of options. After all, these are the mechanisms that acknowledge disparities in educational opportunities, and seek to address them directly. These types of policy must form part of the solution. But they are not the focus of this chapter. Here we'll look at how our arsenal of innovation can be marshalled to aim for the bigger prize: equality of excellence. To succeed here, we would need to design strategies to level up educational standards universally. Achieving equality of excellence would mean that no group of people could gain an advantage (either purposefully or inadvertently) by systematically becoming over-represented at the best schools. No school would be better or worse than another; all schools would be equally excellent.

Really, equality of excellence is the central responsibility of all education secretaries, ministers and administrations the world over – or at least it should be. The fact that this goal is just that, a goal, should serve as a warning that achieving equality of excellence will not be easy.

But we've already seen that there are chinks in the current system's armour. Deprived children are less likely to be taught by fantastic teachers. This is particularly striking as the evidence is clear: great teachers are the most effective lever for increasing educational standards. According to authoritative research organisation the Rand Corporation, 'Teachers matter more to student achievement than any other aspect of schooling'.[15] Adding significant weight to this assertion, John Hattie, a world-renowned educationalist, has demonstrated a) that differences in teacher quality account for 30% of the variation in outcomes between students, b) that teachers are the 'single most powerful influence' in the education system and c) that quality of teaching makes an even bigger difference to a student's outcomes than the nature of a child's home environment.[16]

Meanwhile, the OECD has stressed that the key ingredients needed to make schools both more effective and more equitable include making the teaching profession more attractive to capable individuals, and ensuring that all learners experience high standards of teaching and learning.[17] With the right innovations we can accelerate progress towards these goals. And in achieving these goals, advanced technologies will have made a significant contribution towards enabling equality of excellence throughout the school system.

A great teacher for every single child must be at the centre of any strategy for universal excellence. In this chapter, therefore, we'll explore the ways in which technology can be harnessed to support the efficacy of individual teachers, and upgrade the prestige of the teaching profession as a whole.

Fundamentally, there are two ways in which technology can achieve these goals.[18] Firstly, due to its ability to automate tasks, technology can resolve the problem of unsustainable workloads. The burdens placed upon teachers have led to a recruitment and retention crisis, making it harder to ensure that all learners are taught by great teachers: there simply aren't enough to go around. Technology can add much needed capacity to the teaching profession by automating the repetitive, time-consuming, dull and often low-impact tasks that teachers are currently required to complete. Technology can hence boost the attractiveness of becoming (and remaining) a teacher, hence widening the pool of talented teachers who are available to inspire and develop young people from all backgrounds.[19]

The second reason technology can unlock teachers' full talents and allow them to optimally support learners, is that technology can equip teachers with forensic insights into their learners' needs due to its abilities to capture, process and analyse data at a phenomenal rate. As I'll elaborate, information is a powerful resource. By properly harnessing this information, teaching and learning itself could be upgraded.

In this chapter we'll first explore the problems that technology can solve, and the opportunities it can seize. We'll then turn our attention to how technologies can be applied in the service of equality of excellence.

Unsustainable workload – a problem to solve

Between 2016 and 2017, 10.4% of secondary teachers left the profession.[20] In 2019 the National Education Union found that nearly 20% of teachers were planning to leave the profession in the next two years.[21] This might not be such a critical problem if a healthy supply of new teachers were simultaneously entering the profession. But alas, the UK government has not met its secondary school teacher recruitment targets for seven years running at the time of writing.[22] And all this is unfolding as student numbers continue to rise: the secondary school-age population is forecasted to increase by almost 15% during the next ten years.[23]

A chronic undersupply of teachers is bad news for all pupils, and for society as a whole. But there is also a strong social mobility dimension to this predicament, made clear by the fact that teachers in the most deprived areas are 70% more likely to leave the classroom than teachers in more affluent schools.[24] This indicates that a shortfall in teachers tends to hit the most deprived hardest.

A scarcity of outstanding teachers is both a critical blocker to equality of excellence, and another way in which the dice is loaded against the most disadvantaged. But the flip side of this equation is that focused efforts to get brilliant teachers into the profession – and keep them there – is likely to be most advantageous to the least well off.

Ensuring that students from all socioeconomic backgrounds have access to great teachers is not a new idea by any means. In 2009, the Labour government announced a plan to give excellent teachers a £10,000 bonus for remaining in or moving to schools in disadvantaged areas[25] (the outcome of the 2010 election got in the way slightly). Likewise, Teach First's express purpose is to address educational inequality by 'developing the next generation of great teachers and brilliant leaders'.[26]

These policies and programmes are an important piece of the puzzle; Teach First is particularly close to my heart, as I trained via the Teach First route myself. I fear, however, that by themselves these approaches won't address all the root causes of the problem.

The National Education Union has highlighted exactly why teachers are leaving the profession in droves: unsustainable workloads.[27] On average, teachers put in 54.4 hours a week,[28] which equates to 43% more time than a typical 38-hour week. Moreover, a quarter of teachers work more than sixty hours per week.[29] A study by The National Foundation for Educational Research has shown that even when taking into account school holidays, teachers are still significantly overworked.[30]

The Department for Education's 2016 Teacher Workload Survey[31] gives non-teachers line of sight into how a teacher's time is apportioned. The survey shows that full-time classroom teachers spend on average 20.7 hours teaching and 34.2 hours on non-teaching tasks. The most time-consuming set of tasks outside of the classroom is 'planning or preparation of lessons either at school or out-of-school', which weighed in at 8.8 hours. After planning, the second most time-consuming non-teaching task was 'marking/correcting pupils' work' (8.1 hours), with general administration coming in third (4.1 hours).

Focusing on marking/correcting pupils' work, this is a necessary component of good teaching as it allows teachers to mine for valuable information about their learners' needs.[32] But is the amount of time teachers are spending on such tasks worth the diminished work/life balance and heightened levels of stress, which ultimately leads to a lack of good teachers in the profession? And do teachers really get enough valuable information from this process to justify the time spent? Perhaps not. In 2016, the UK government published a report by the Independent Teacher Workload Review Group entitled *Eliminating unnecessary workload around marking*. The report identified that 53% of respondents to an official survey agreed that 'whilst marking pupils' work is necessary and productive, the excessive nature, depth and frequency of marking was burdensome.' The report itself acknowledged that although marking was a 'vital element' of teaching and learning, it could also be ineffective and therefore constitute a waste of teachers' valuable time. Bad practices were highlighted, such as giving extensive written feedback on all or most of learners' work, and also cultures in schools and colleges that drive teachers towards ever-increasing quantities of marking even when it is ineffective and unneeded. But the report also makes clear why some amount of marking is needed. At its best, marking enables teachers to provide tailored support for each learner. Key to effective marking is that teachers are taking in information about how individual students are learning and progressing as an input, and are then making decisions on how to best support each student as an output. Teachers who are pushed to write comments next to every bit of work that a pupil does are not necessarily realising this ideal.[33]

To retain excellent teachers, attract a wealth of talent into the profession and get the best out of everyone, unsustainable workloads have to be addressed. But simply decreeing that teachers no longer have to mark work, analyse data or complete administrative tasks might not be the best solution for learners. This problem requires a novel solution.

Empowered with information – an opportunity to seize

Information is to education as oxygen is to organic life. In their authoritative paper *Inside the Black Box*,[34] eminent educationalists Paul Black and Dylan Wiliam stress that:

> …a teacher's approach should start by being realistic and confronting the question, 'Do I really know enough about the understanding of my pupils to be able to help each of them?'

As Black and Wiliam make clear, information is a necessary component of teaching and learning because teachers (and learners themselves) must constantly make decisions about how best to aid learning. How can I stretch this pupil? How do I address that misconception? At what point should we move on to the next topic? How else can I explain this concept? What activity will support learners to develop these skills further? What questions should I ask to interrogate and develop this learner's understanding? How can I support this pupil pastorally? How can I motivate these learners? How can I ensure they are engaged and inspired?

To answer these questions – and many more like them – teachers need to thoroughly understand how their students' knowledge, understanding and skill sets are developing. More importantly, they need to understand their students as people. In short, they need as much information as they can possibly digest. And this includes information relating to their own practice. John Hattie has demonstrated that effective teachers also need to gather and evaluate information about the impact that their decisions and actions are having. Teachers need such information to truly understand how teaching is influencing learning, which in turn allows them to adapt and optimise their practice.[35]

Black and Wiliam's groundbreaking work has led to the practice of formative assessment becoming mainstream. Formative assessment, which refers to the process of informally assessing pupil performance in detail and acting upon the resulting information to better support students, has reimagined the role of the teacher; they have gone from being the 'sage on the stage' to the 'guide on the side'.[36] In days gone by, the teacher standing at the blackboard may have seen little sense in devoting time to developing a deep understanding of how his or her pupils' knowledge, skills and understanding were progressing. The teacher was there to teach; the students were there to learn. At the end of each year, students might be summatively assessed through formal examinations (either internal or external). But such processes provided little opportunity to correct misunderstandings, accelerate skill development and ensure optimal progress for learners on an ongoing basis. Summative assessments provide a means of measuring knowledge, skills and understanding that have already been developed. Formative assessments, on the other hand, provide a means of strategically developing knowledge, skills and understanding further still. And what does formative assessment rely on? Information.

Black and Wiliam have emphasised that when teachers adopt this teaching method effectively, the impact on students is so significant that, if made prevalent throughout the school system, it could result in the equivalent of raising the overall mathematics scores of pupils in England (an average-performing education system) to levels achieved in the top five performing education systems in the world.[37] This is testament to the fact that information is one of the most powerful resources that teachers (and learners themselves) have at their disposal.

There are numerous ways in which teachers extract information on individuals' learning and develop a picture of their strengths and needs. Marking learners' work is one example. But here, the time lag between a student completing their work, a teacher marking the work and the student responding to the marking[38] means that marking is not always the most effective way to address learners' needs in the short term.[39] Questioning pupils directly is a more immediate method that teachers can apply. Effective questions can be designed to give teachers a clear idea of learners' skills, from recall all the way up to higher order thinking skills[40] such as evaluation. Alternatively, if students were engaged in collaborative project-based tasks, for instance, a teacher might choose to traverse the classroom, listening to and analysing the discussions taking place. From the information gathered, the teacher would be able to decide which students needed support, and what support they needed. In other contexts, some teachers will use mini-whiteboards to gain information about how well learners have understood a particular point. With this technique, a teacher might ask a question but instead of getting just one pupil to come to the board or put their hand up to provide an answer, the whole class writes down their answer on the mini-whiteboard. This gives teachers a snapshot of where the whole class is at, rather than insight into only one student.

Teachers are not just applying formative assessment techniques to find out if pupils know the right answer. They are also trying to find out why they gave the response they did and how well they understood the broader topic. In practice, this means using a range of assessment techniques in quick succession; the more information the better.

In addition to formative assessment, giving tailored feedback is a related teaching practice that is also fuelled by information. The Educational Endowment Foundation, a charity that works towards 'breaking the link between family income and educational achievement'[41] by providing educators with evidence-based solutions to improve learner performance, has shown that providing quality feedback is the single most powerful utility in a teacher's toolkit. According to their definition:

> Feedback is information given to the learner or teacher about the learner's performance relative to learning goals or outcomes. It should aim towards (and be capable of producing) improvement in students' learning. Feedback redirects or refocuses either the teacher's or the learner's actions to achieve a goal, by aligning effort and activity with an outcome.[42]

Providing quality feedback that allows learners to better achieve positive outcomes, relies on information about learning and teaching. Acting decisively and effectively on this information can make a real difference to learning and to learners' life chances. The evidence suggests that by consistently utilising information about learning and the impacts of teaching, learners' GCSEs could be boosted by half a grade per subject.[43] Elsewhere, it has been shown that using information to understand the progress that students are making can help to achieve gains in teaching quality.[44]

These positives aside, there are natural limits to the amount of information teachers can extract and analyse. Technology will not make teachers' abilities boundless, but it can significantly enhance teaching and learning by increasing the levels of information that teachers have access to.

Technology in action

We already have a sizeable toolbox of innovations that can help to address unsustainable workloads and empower teachers with key insights into the needs of their learners. In many cases, technologies are able to kill two birds with one stone by first automating the time consuming and monotonous tasks of marking work and inputting data, and then giving teachers the end product – a wealth of information about their pupils' learning – on a plate. Flipped learning provides a key example of how this principle can work in practice.[45] Flipped learning is a simple yet powerful teaching method. Students learn the basics of a topic before a lesson, then, when in the classroom, they apply and extend what they have learned. To illustrate, when learning about the generation of electricity, learners may be set a homework task whereby they learn about and complete an assessment on different types of power plant. This task might be intended to get learners to a point where they can identify and describe different methods of generating electricity, from wind farms to nuclear power plants. In the subsequent lesson, students could progress further by applying their knowledge to devise an energy strategy for a hypothetical society, which would require evaluating the features of different power plants in relation to the needs and characteristics of the society. This task could even involve presenting, debating or writing persuasively, and, therefore, develop learners' skills holistically.

This method is called flipped learning because it inverts the more traditional practice of using homework to extend learning on a topic that was first introduced in the classroom. With flipped learning, educators don't have to just assume that the prerequisite learning has taken place before the lesson. From their perspective, the lynchpin that drives flipped learning is the information they receive about how well learners have performed in their initial home learning task. With the example above, teachers would be provided with information on the extent to which each student can define, identify and describe different ways of generating electricity. With this information, the teacher can then identify which ideas have been grasped by students, and where there are still gaps. The teacher will also be able to see which students need additional support and which students need to be challenged further. They could even use this information to decide on groupings for collaborative tasks.[46]

Flipped learning gets results. In a project led by Shireland Collegiate Academy, an innovative research school in the West Midlands, a flipped learning programme for primary school pupils called MathsFlip resulted in the equivalent of one month's extra progress per year, rising to an extra two months' progress per year for the most disadvantaged pupils. Twenty-four primary schools took part in the evaluation, and the project was independently evaluated by the Institute for Effective Education.[47]

In 2015, a leading academic suggested that schools should consider outsourcing marking to countries such as India because workload had become so unsustainable.[48] But this would not be necessary if students and teachers were routinely benefiting from flipped learning programmes. With such programmes, online platforms can be used to mark pupils' responses automatically; and then collate, analyse and present the resultant information – the all-important end product of marking – which teachers can subsequently use to tailor their next lesson to the specific needs of the learners in their class.

Automated marking needn't be reserved for work done at home, however. Platforms such as CENTURY (which we'll explore in more depth momentarily) are used as part of blended lessons as well as for homework.[49] As students learn via CENTURY, teachers themselves learn about their students' needs. As CENTURY Tech (the company behind the innovative platform) explains:

> The platform gathers data insights about each student, including their achievement, knowledge, skills and performance against assessment objectives, which are presented back to the teacher in real-time via easy to use dashboards. This data enables teachers to deliver timely, targeted interventions and to employ evidence based teaching strategies.[50]

As well as supplying teachers with vital insights into their students' needs, CENTURY also reduces teacher workload significantly. Teachers who use the platform have reported that CENTURY saves them six hours a week on average.[51]

Other technological solutions also enable teachers to make better use of less time. Bolton College uses a digital assistant called Ada (named after Ada Lovelace) to support the day-to-day operations of the college. Ada caught the attention of then Education Secretary Damian Hinds who gave the following praise:

'Ada helps deliver personalised learning and assessment for 14,000 students [and] queries about attendance or curriculum content.

'It has saved Bolton's staff hours and hours of time they would have spent on admin either at college or in their own spare time.

'This is showing tech at its most transformative and enabling.'[52]

The architect behind Ada has explained that digital assistants could potentially be used to collate weekly reports for individual students.[53] In a traditional school model, teachers tend to put together annual (or perhaps termly) reports for students, which can be a useful means of recognising students' achievements and reaching mutual decisions on focal points for improvement. Manually creating a report each week would be incredibly taxing for teachers, but automated weekly reports could be hugely beneficial as they would facilitate fine-grained support for each learner.

Technology's ability to automate not only results in a net reduction in workload for teachers, it actually allows them to spend their time in a more fulfilling way (which includes maintaining a sustainable work-life balance). Learners therefore immediately benefit from teachers who are less burdened by the stress of being overworked and who have the time to address their individual needs more effectively. The long-term benefits experienced by learners could be greater still as the reduction in mundane tasks, and the heightened focus on pedagogical skill, increases the attractiveness of the teaching profession and enables more young people to be taught by inspiring teachers.

But what about the workload involved in marking essays or extended written answers? Can technology automate away the time teachers currently spend on these tasks? Maybe.

In January 2020, Ofqual – the organisation responsible for regulating assessments, examinations and qualifications in England – announced that it would be exploring the potential use of AI for supporting the marking of students' assessments.[54] The underlying motivation for this exploration was not workload but accuracy. Pointing to research around AI's efficacy in breast cancer screenings, which suggests that AI can be more effective at identifying cases of breast cancer than a single doctor, Ofqual suggested that AI could potentially be used as either a 'second marker' or a means of monitoring and improving the quality of marking. To help them understand how AI could fulfil these roles effectively, Ofqual announced an upcoming 'AI competition' to build software that could mark students' essays accurately.

It should be reiterated that the motivation behind using AI within the exam-marking process was not to reduce teacher workload, but to improve accuracy. Outside of the exam-marking context, this is especially important to remember because interacting with students' written work is a crucial part of teaching (though it isn't necessarily as important for summative assessments). As part of day-to-day teaching and learning, and in the spirit of formative assessment, teachers do need to take time to digest students' thoughts, perspectives and arguments, which are far too subtle, nuanced and unique to be entirely captured by a machine. There is hence a limit to the benefits of automated essay-marking. That said, some automation of essay-marking would have positive impacts that could make all the difference for learners. A year-11 student preparing for their history GCSE exam, for instance, might want to practise writing essays and then get a broad indication of their performance. As it stands, teachers cannot be expected to mark every single piece of work interminably, as there simply aren't enough hours in the day. This creates a hold-up. The student wants some level of feedback on all their practice essays in order to understand their strengths and areas for development. But with time being a scarce resource, there is no guarantee that they will receive feedback at the rate they desire. An automated essay-marking tool could change this. With such a tool the student could complete a number of practice essays, have them marked automatically, and then find time to sit down with a teacher to understand and improve upon their overall performance. From a broader perspective, McKinsey has discussed the use of innovations that can monitor ongoing trends in the quality of students' written work, and provide more targeted feedback.[55] Such innovations could enable teachers to have oversight of students' learning, and hence make regular, well-informed interventions to focus on individual students.

Moving away from the theme of reducing teacher workload briefly, there is another way in which automated marking could boost social mobility: by facilitating reforms to university admissions. Under the current admissions system, university offers are primarily made on the basis of a student's predicted grades, despite the fact that these predictions are only right 16% of the time.[56] This means that if your grades are under-predicted you may miss out on an offer from a top university, even if you go on to secure the grades that you would have needed to meet such an offer. This harms social mobility because less advantaged students are far more likely to have their grades under-predicted.[57] An obvious solution would be to scrap the current system and no longer rely on predicted grades when offering places at universities. Such a solution may be on the cards. At the time of writing, the Education Secretary, Gavin Williamson, has recently announced that his department will be 'exploring how best to transform the admission process' and will be consulting on a post-qualifications admissions system.[58] There are both benefits and challenges to this approach. While commending the advantages of a post-qualifications admissions system, the General Secretary for the Association of School and College Leaders (ASCL) has previously explained that:

> It would be extremely difficult to manage the entire applications process in the few weeks between A-level results in mid-August and the beginning of university terms in September or October, and it is likely that we would need to rethink the entire calendar.[59]

But if automated essay-marking software can demonstrate that it is accurate and fair, these tools could make the applications process much easier to manage. Scrapping predicted grades could hence become viable. This should lead to fewer disadvantaged students missing out on the places they deserve due to inaccurate forecasts of their future grades.

Moving back to teacher workload – currently too much of teachers' time is spent harvesting information when they should be focusing their time on putting that information to use by making insight-driven decisions about how best to support their students. Together, marking and general administration currently account for 12.2 hours of an average teacher's weekly workload. But this situation is not inevitable. As previously noted, there are teachers who are already saving six hours per week by using CENTURY. This equates to more than a 10% reduction in a teacher's working week.[60] McKinsey estimates that an even higher proportion of teachers' time could ultimately be saved if schools made full use of the digital resources that are available. They estimate that teachers currently spend 20-40% of their time on tasks that could be automated by technologies that already exist.[61] Not only will this make teachers' workloads more manageable, it will also make the role of a teacher far more enjoyable as a greater proportion of a teacher's time will be spent doing the more fulfilling aspects of the role. Indeed, if up to 40% of the tasks teachers are currently doing are automated, then, as McKinsey notes, there will be increased time for highly rewarding tasks such as delivering 'more personalized learning and more direct coaching and mentoring'.[62] As job satisfaction rises, teacher recruitment and retention rates will follow suit. An abundance of excellent teachers will stream into schools, which will raise educational standards, particularly in the schools most adversely affected by current teacher shortages.

But be warned. Yes, giving teachers their lives back and allowing them to spend a greater proportion of the working day on the most fulfilling aspects of the job could reverse the recruitment and retention crisis, and ensure a strong pipeline of talent enters and stays in the profession. But the gains made through purposeful uses of technology could easily be squandered due to poor governance. Unsustainable workloads are not the only reason teachers are leaving the profession in droves, unable to be replaced. Intrusive levels of monitoring and 'punitive' accountability regimes have also been shown to be significant contributing factors.[63] Teachers are highly skilled professionals and deserve to be treated as such. Yes, there need to be systems in place to ensure the overall quality of teaching is sufficiently high enough to meet learners' needs, but teachers are better placed to achieve these high standards when they are able to exercise their own professional judgements without being under intensive surveillance. Well-deployed technologies will improve the job description, but it's up to school leaders to secure the best possible working environment.

Then there's the elephant in the room: pay. As I have made clear, fantastic teachers make all the difference to children's life chances. Their pay should reflect this. The pledge made by the Conservative government in their 2019 manifesto to increase teachers' starting salaries to £30,000[64] is welcomed and may have a sizeable positive impact on teacher recruitment in its own right. Governments will need to make good on their promises to pay teachers what they deserve in order to ensure that young people from all backgrounds are exclusively taught by excellent teachers.

All things being equal, students stand to gain immeasurably and equitably from targeted innovations that result in a plentiful supply of excellent, well-resourced teachers. But this only gets us to the foothills of what can be achieved with the help of technology. Outside of the classroom, technologies earn their keep by automating tasks that don't necessarily require a teacher's talents to complete. But inside the classroom, teachers are indispensable: here technology's role is hence to augment and amplify their talents.

To illustrate, let's consider how technology can enhance collaborative learning.[65] Imagine a classroom where thirty students are engaged in project-based group work. The learners are working collaboratively to resolve a hypothetical society's energy crisis, and then present their solutions to the class. As well as enabling students to develop and apply their scientific understanding, this kind of activity requires students to use critical thinking, alongside listening and communication skills. The design of effective collaborative learning activities relies upon teachers' expert pedagogical skills. But as well as writing the symphony, teachers are also required to conduct the orchestra by overseeing and supporting students during such tasks.[66] But how should they use their time most effectively? Which groups need their support and who would benefit more from a hands-off approach? Where a student needs a helping hand, what support do they actually need? Having to deal with incomplete information, a teacher's interventions will inevitably be suboptimal. It should be clear what role technology has to play. Enter intelligent moderation.

The following explanation, provided in *Intelligence Unleashed*, gives a clear sense of how intelligent moderation can add value and of what it can achieve.

With large student numbers working in multiple collaborative groups, it can be impossible for a person to make any sense of the large volume of data that the participants are generating in their discussions.

Intelligent moderation uses AI techniques such as machine learning and shallow text processing to analyse and summarise the discussions to enable a human tutor to guide the students towards fruitful collaboration. For example, the system might provide alerts to human tutors to inform them of significant events (such as students going off topic or repeating misconceptions) that may require their intervention or support.[67]

While intelligent moderation has been employed within online discussions, with learners' written interactions acting as the key source of data,[68] the principles underlying intelligent moderation can be readily transferred to real-life classrooms. Indeed, AI tools that take in data on students' nonverbal interactions during group-based problem-solving activities are already able to evaluate students' competence in these tasks. As demonstrated by a team of researchers at University College London and the University of Malaga, this is because individual students' body language and the ways in which whole groups interact non-verbally can provide valuable information regarding how well students are working together.[69]

Teachers will be empowered in two distinct respects by the timely insights coming from intelligent moderation tools used in the classroom. As overall directors of their lessons and managers of the resources at their disposal, teachers will be equipped with increased levels of information with which to make strategic decisions about how best to apportion their time.[70] As the most powerful resource[71] in the classroom (except perhaps the students themselves), their interactions with individual students will be enhanced as they will have a better understanding of each person's needs.

Intelligent moderators are not acting as automators. Their purpose is to extract insight from data, which teachers can then use to enhance their practice. Teachers are still responsible for deciding how best to use their time during the lesson, and it is they who will take action wherever it is needed. The core responsibilities have not been reallocated at all. The technology is there to inform teachers' decisions and sharpen their interventions.[72] It adds value because it distils a barrage of useful information into a digestible format at a rate that humans could never achieve. Recall the pivotal question posed to teachers by Dylan Wiliam and Paul Black: 'Do I really know enough about the understanding of my pupils to be able to help each of them?' Technology's aptitude to extract insights from data on students' learning will usher in a paradigm shift in how well teachers can grasp their students' understanding. Artificial intelligence (AI) will be at the forefront of this paradigm shift.

As one of the world's foremost experts on AI in education, Professor Rose Luckin has argued that artificial intelligence can 'open up the "black box of learning"'.[73] By processing large amounts of data related to students' learning, AI tools allow teachers and students to see the learning process under a magnifying glass. This allows teachers to provide more tailored support to students as and when they need it, and it also means that teachers can develop a more robust, long-term understanding of how each child learns and what further intervention they may need.[74] Yet again, teachers are empowered to be better directors of learning and equipped to deliver sharper interventions, enhancing both their strategic and tactical prowess.

It should also be emphasised that obtaining deep insights into learners' needs doesn't require devices to constantly be used as the primary mode of learning. As we have already seen with the example of collaborative learning, technology can significantly aid teaching and learning without intruding upon the more personal aspects of education, which are crucial for a learner's well-rounded development. The necessary software can stay backstage, obligingly capturing data through sensors, microphones, cameras, etc., as students learn.[75]

In this respect, as well as supporting teachers to understand their students, technologies could also allow teachers to better understand their own teaching practice. This would help teachers to make informed decisions on how to adapt aspects of their teaching and support their students optimally.

From my own experience as a science teacher, one of the most useful professional development programmes I ever engaged in was peer-coaching. All teachers at the secondary school in which I taught were given two hours a week to devote to the programme – which, I must assert, is not a typical school policy. One hour would be spent observing a colleague and evaluating a particular aspect of their teaching (reciprocally, they would spend one of their allotted hours observing you). The other hour was used to evaluate both of your lessons in depth. During one cycle, I had asked a colleague to focus on how well differentiated my use of questioning was. Was I asking the right types of questions to stretch and challenge students? Was I distributing my questions evenly among students in the class? To help me answer these questions and more, my colleague would record every question I asked and categorise it based on the level of challenge. A closed question would generally be a low level of challenge, and a question that required deeper levels of analysis would generally be considered more challenging. This level of support allowed me to reflect on my teaching and make well-informed judgements on how I could improve.

Ideally, coaching programmes would be made widely available to all teachers. But even if such programmes were prevalently used in schools, AI-based emulations of coaching would be extraordinarily valuable as they would be able to provide insights to teachers on not just one lesson a week – or even less frequently – but on every lesson they taught. As Hattie has shown, teachers are at their most effective when they are constantly evaluating which interactions with students have the greatest impact. By analysing the impact of different teaching approaches, AI can empower teachers to develop, refine and improve their practice. Innovative lesson observation system Lessonvu already utilises AI to enable teachers to evaluate and improve upon their own teaching practice in a way that is non-intrusive.[76]

As well as equipping teachers with valuable insights, intelligent analytics can also be used at an institutional level to provide learners with targeted support. A model to build upon is provided by Georgia State University's Graduation and Progression Success (GPS) system, which uses predictive analytics to identify students who are at risk of not successfully graduating. Since being operationalised, the GPS system has supported tens of thousands of at-risk students. The system flagged these individuals as being at risk and they were hence given tailored, in-person support to help them get 'back on track'.[77] By allowing these students to get the support they needed at a time when interventions could still make a difference, the GPS system has contributed to improved academic performance for students, particularly among those from low-income households and minority backgrounds;[78] the system has also facilitated a 5% increase in student retention.[79] Underneath the bonnet, the system works because it had analysed historical data from approximately 2.5 million students who attended the university over a ten-year period. From this data, the system unearthed patterns that were used to predict which students were most at risk of not graduating.[80]

Transposing this model to compulsory education, schools could adopt similar tools to predict students who are at risk of not achieving particular benchmarks. For instance, schools could use historical data to predict students at risk of not achieving a 'good pass' in GCSE English and maths (grades required for a significant proportion of jobs), or – if student destination data is properly recorded – schools could even use predictive analytics to identify students at risk of long periods of unemployment. Such predictions could enable schools to use resources effectively to prevent any student from being left behind. This positive outcome will depend, however, on how effectively educators use the newly available information. As advisers rather than automators, the technologies employed are not ultimately responsible for the final outcome: people are.

So far, we have seen that technologies can enhance and amplify the power of teachers. Enriched levels of information on the collective needs of the whole class can enable better planning and orchestration of lessons,[81] and deep insights into individual needs can allow teachers to tailor the interventions they provide in aid of particular students. A critical problem, however, is that the time that teachers (as managers) have to deploy themselves (as resources) to support individual students is limited. Equipping teachers with the information needed to support students individually is all very well, but if there simply isn't time for teachers to provide direct support then there is a real risk that much of this information will just go to waste. Fortunately, teachers have resources other than themselves to deploy.

Personalised, responsive learning at scale

Evidence from the Education Endowment Foundation (EEF) demonstrates that individualised learning – whereby teachers provide learners with different tasks and interventions based on their own needs – leads, on average, to the equivalent of three months of additional progress for students.[82] Despite its benefits, however, individualised (or personalised) learning is hard to sustain. Instead of planning and preparing materials for a single 'one-size-fits-all'[83] lesson, to achieve individualised levels of instruction teachers often need to prepare for two, three, four or more lessons, which will all take place simultaneously. Consider also that a teacher's ability to deliver fine-grained interventions responsively is critically limited due to time constraints and student-teacher ratios.

These problems provide us with one prism through which to understand the benefits to be gained from advanced technologies that support learners directly. Such technologies enable teachers to deliver personalised learning in a sustainable way, and they can also enhance the efficacy of this teaching method. As shown by the EEF, modes of individualised learning that make use of digital technologies tend to be more effective than those that don't. A key factor here is that technologies can enable immediate feedback for students.[84]

Adaptive technologies enable individualised learning on steroids[85]. Rather than differentiating for a small number of key groupings of students, digital resources allow for genuine individual-level customisation of learning.[86] And instead of students waiting long periods to receive feedback on their work, adaptive technologies can be so responsive that students are able to benefit from feedback and additional support immediately.[87]

CENTURY is a pioneering platform that uses machine learning algorithms to personalise learning[88] 'for each and every student'.[89] The platform can identify every student's strengths and areas for development[90] and, drawing upon a 'rich data store', CENTURY is able to provide tailored support for individual students.[91] The educational content that students access on the platform is created by experienced teachers,[92] who have structured the curriculum into micro-lessons called 'nuggets'.[93] Armed with innovative software and exceptional learning material, CENTURY is able to recommend 'the most useful nugget... at exactly the right time'.[94] By using the platform, every student in a class can experience a learning journey that is uniquely personalised to them. And as part of this journey, students can receive immediate feedback to further support their learning.[95]

As well as empowering learners, CENTURY also empowers teachers. As students learn on CENTURY, teachers are able to monitor progress in real time via the platform's teacher dashboards.[96] This allows teachers to identify how to best support each student, enabling them to provide an additional rich layer of personalisation to students' learning.[97]

As I've emphasised, information is central to teaching and learning. The ability of adaptive learning platforms to provide teachers with in-depth information about students' learning is hence just as important as the responsiveness and granularity of these platforms. But teachers aren't the only beneficiaries of rich insights into students' learning. By using adaptive learning platforms, students themselves benefit immensely from insights that enable them to reflect on and further promote their progress.[98] A further benefit of these platforms, therefore, is that they can be used to open up the black box of learning for students as well as for teachers.[99] Through the use of AI, students can gain a deeper understanding of their levels of knowledge and comprehension across different topic areas. They could even be given oversight of their development with regards to more fundamental skills, such as collaboration, persistence, confidence and motivation.[100] Adaptive learning platforms can therefore facilitate greater levels of independence and introspection, which are among the most important attributes any young person needs to develop in order to flourish throughout their lives.

AI-enabled adaptive learning platforms are one of the most powerful digital tools that teachers and learners have at their disposal. Their combined ability to draw out deep insights into learners' needs and then to intervene responsively, means that students are able to experience personalised learning at a scale that would not otherwise have been possible.

Another way in which some of the most advanced platforms empower learners and teachers alike is by commandeering expertise from domains such as neuroscience and psychology, therefore enabling fine-tuned pedagogical approaches that would be particularly difficult for teachers to deliver without additional support.[101]

MyCognition, for instance, 'enhances cognitive fitness through a structured programme of insight, assessment and training'.[102] One way in which users benefit from MyCognition is through scientifically designed games, which are customised to each individual's needs and used to train and prime cognitive fitness.[103] With improved cognitive fitness comes enhancements to a person's memory, reasoning skills and ability to adapt to new situations.[104] As stated on the NHS website, MyCognition (specifically referring to the app, MyCognition Home) can help its users 'think faster, focus better, and improve decision-making and memory'.[105] A study into MyCognition's impact in schools has shown that spending sixty minutes or more a week training via MyCognition can lead to significant improvements in students' cognitive fitness – improvements that have been linked to further benefits, including improvements in maths and writing skills.[106]

Without such highly specialised solutions, it would be difficult for students to experience the benefits of cognitive training: an in-depth understanding of cognitive fitness is not necessarily within the skill set of all teachers. Purposeful innovations should hence be deployed to bring new expertise relevant to learning and development into the classroom (and beyond).

This principle can also be seen in HegartyMaths' use of behavioural insights. HegartyMaths, a mathematics platform co-founded by award-winning teacher Colin Hegarty,[107] applies behavioural insights to prompt students to get help when they get a question wrong. Before introducing these techniques, the team at HegartyMaths identified that students were making use of the 'Get Help' button, which supports students by allowing them to see a worked example of a similar mathematical problem to ones they have answered incorrectly, with insufficient frequency.[108] As noted in the report *Applying Behavioural Insights in EdTech: An incomplete guide,* co-authored by Nesta, HegartyMaths and the Behavioural Insights Team, this support feature has been described as 'the closest thing you could get to having a teacher standing beside a student, helping them if they made a mistake'; as such, HegartyMaths resolved to address this issue by finding innovative ways to encourage students to get help. Working alongside Nesta and the Behavioral Insights Team (AKA the Nudge Unit),[109] HegartyMaths adapted the process for getting help in such a way as to reduce the 'friction cost' (the 'hassle' and effort associated with more cumbersome tasks) for students. Instead of having to actively click out of a particular task in order to get help, students were prompted to get help via timely pop-ups. This increased the rate at which students asked for help by over 100%.[110]

AI can also be purposefully utilised to support the learning of languages. The Tactical Language and Culture Training System (TLCTS), for instance, employs speech-recognition software to support those learning foreign languages.[111] On the TLCTS, learners can interact with 'virtual humans', which enables 'extensive conversational practice'.[112] Developed by pioneering company Alelo, the system is in widespread use among military personnel, who often need to be proficient in foreign languages.[113]

Technologies that utilise speech recognition techniques can also be applied to develop users' communication skills. Gweek analyses how a person communicates and hence supports users to become more effective at interacting with people.[114] Gweek can be used in professional contexts,[115] and this innovation can also be applied in the classroom.[116] By helping learners to develop this vital skillset, Gweek provides robust grounds for optimism that artificial intelligence will not only support students to learn existing content more effectively, AI could also enable students to develop a more rounded set of proficiencies.

From the above discussion it should be clear that advanced technologies that support learners directly have an important role to play in achieving equality of excellence. That said, we must remember that technology does not have a monopoly on personalised, responsive learning. Empowered by both rich insights into learners' needs and time carved out in their diaries, teachers should be able to offer an additional layer of personalisation.[117]

As the EEF has shown, one-to-one tuition delivered by an experienced teacher can yield the equivalent of five months of additional progress for learners, making it among the most powerful interventions a school can deliver.[118] Experienced teachers need to be optimally utilised if such gains are to be made routinely. As I have already noted, McKinsey predicts that, thanks to the application of technology, teachers will have more time to spend on activities such as 'direct coaching and mentoring'.[119] In order to support their students optimally, all schools should voraciously take up this opportunity. Students should be able to systematically benefit from meaningful levels of focused support in the form of one-to-one tuition delivered by an inspiring teacher (and at a reasonable frequency).

This point brings us back to where we left off at the end of the previous chapter. As a reminder, I made the point that the ultimate way to eliminate inequalities in the shadow education system would be to bring this sector into the light, integrating it with the formal education system. We are now in a position to get a tangible sense of how this would work. Through the lens of the shadow education system, ITSs are an adjunct to the school system. They are resources that learners make use of entirely of their own volition, via which they follow an educational pathway that is not necessarily bound to what they were studying in school. But through the lens of a universally excellent school system, these resources – whether they're referred to as ITSs or adaptive learning platforms – can be more powerful still. Students can utilise the same high-quality resources at home as they do during a proportion of their lessons. Teachers can guide students as to what aspects of the curriculum to focus on during independent sessions – which could take place at home, or perhaps in spaces such as the school's library.[120] And by making use of their dashboards, teachers can gain insights into how students are progressing as they learn independently. Teachers may even be able to conduct bespoke one-to-one sessions with students, in which the teacher could review what the student has been learning in their own time. As a result, the shadow education system could become wholly irrelevant and utterly incapable of conferring any advantage upon those who choose to access private tuition in addition to formal education.

The Fourth Education Revolution

Up to this point we have considered the potential impact of utilising existing and emerging technologies within our current education system. But it would be naive to think that innovations are not capable of leading to deeper structural changes. In his book, *The Fourth Education Revolution*,[121] Sir Anthony Seldon argues that the widespread application of artificial intelligence and other advanced technologies will precipitate a paradigm shift in how people are educated. Note that under this model our current education system was brought about by the third education revolution, which saw access to schools and universities being opened up, rather than being almost exclusively for the elites. Of particular importance to our discussion, he also argues that this anticipated paradigm shift will be a boon for social mobility.

Seldon argues that within the new paradigm, learning will be significantly more focused on the needs of individuals, students will develop a broader range of skills and intelligences, and exams will be replaced by online continuous assessments. According to Seldon, teachers will be an enduring necessity after the fourth education revolution, though their roles - being more strategic, pastoral and geared towards the well-rounded development of students - will change immeasurably and for the better. As well as spending less time on menial, administrative tasks (something that, as we have seen, can already be achieved), teachers will devote fewer hours to preparing/curating resources and presenting content.

Significantly, it is argued that there is no danger of schools themselves becoming redundant in the future due to the fact that education is an inherently social activity. That said, traditional classrooms may be unnecessary in the future, as more flexible learning spaces become favoured, with Seldon suggesting that libraries may be the focal spaces in schools.

The case is explicitly made that the fourth education revolution will boost social mobility. According to Seldon, universal access to personalised learning will directly address the fact that currently those from higher socioeconomic backgrounds are likely to benefit from smaller class sizes and experience a better quality of teaching and learning.

I am personally inspired by the promise of greater levels of personalisation, blended in with the more cohesive, sociable aspects of learning; and I am excited by the prospect of learners' skills, competencies and personalities being developed in a more holistic, well-rounded way. Where I differ slightly with Sir Anthony, however, is in one aspect of his diagnosis of our current educational paradigm, which he argues is beset by a number of 'intractable problems'. While

I entirely agree that teachers are systematically overwhelmed by mountainous workloads, and that a broad and personalised approach to learning is difficult to achieve at present, I am optimistic that some version of our current education system could overcome deep-rooted social immobility. In my opinion, the current system is not beyond repair, though it does need to evolve if it is to achieve equality of excellence. If a young person from a disadvantaged background is fortunate enough to go to one of the UK's many outstanding schools (note it is not a rare occurrence for top schools to have inclusive intakes, though it is far too uncommon) then social immobility may not seem like such an intractable problem from their perspective – if you put to one side the obstacles that schools cannot address by themselves, that is (more on this point later).

As we've seen, going to a great school and being taught by fantastic teachers can have significant positive impacts on all learners, regardless of their background. Therefore, in my view, the central problem with the current system is that there is a scarcity of great schools, staffed invariably by inspiring teachers. Because outstanding schools do exist within our current paradigm (both in the UK and globally), I question whether a revolution is required to lift other schools up to the same high standard. That said, significant structural changes are sorely needed in order to achieve high quality with consistency. Whether change should happen via evolution or revolution is perhaps a matter of semantics; the important thing is that it does happen. The vision of the fourth education revolution serves as a north star, guiding societies towards an education system that is fairer, more fulfilling, and fundamentally respectful of teaching and learning as a human endeavour. In progressing towards this destination, I see technology's role as being to accentuate the best aspects of our current education systems. I am particularly excited about technology's ability to enhance the relationship between students and teachers, and to strengthen the potency of the most effective aspects of teaching: feedback and formative assessment, collaborative learning, differentiation, and more. Therefore, as the uptake of technology accelerates, the priority in my view should be to purposefully utilise technologies to ensure that every child is taught by an inspiring, well-resourced and time-rich teacher.

CHAPTER 5

ACHIEVING A DYNAMIC AND INCLUSIVE WORKFORCE

In the UK, a person's background significantly influences their career trajectory. This is particularly evident in the dominance of privately educated individuals in the elite professions. The Sutton Trust and the Social Mobility Commission have demonstrated that 39% of people in the most elite professions were educated privately despite the fact that in total, only 7% of Britons were. This means that those born into the wealthiest households are over-represented in the top professions almost by a factor of six[1] (5.6 to be exact). And with the over-representation of privately educated individuals in the professions comes the concomitant under-representation of everyone else. If the top 7% get 39% of the pie, then the bottom 93% must make do with 61% of the pie – which is just under two thirds as big a slice as you would expect them to get if equality of opportunity reigned throughout the land. The divide between state-educated and privately educated students is only part of the story, however. Looking more broadly, the Social Mobility Commission has shown that people from more affluent backgrounds are 80% more likely to enter professional roles, compared to those from less advantaged backgrounds.[2]

But Britain's socially immobile labour market is not just a moral problem; it is an economic problem too. And given the calamitous impacts of the Covid-19 pandemic, the economy urgently needs revivifying. Focused efforts to boost social mobility could be an important part of the solution. The Sutton Trust and the Boston Consulting Group have calculated that significantly increasing social mobility in the UK could expand the economy by £140 billion a year by 2050, equivalent to an additional 4% growth in GDP. In total this would mean £1.3 trillion in additional income during the first half of this century.[3] A further report authored by Oxera and prepared for The Sutton Trust calculated that modestly increasing the UK's levels of social mobility to the Western European average could add 2% to GDP, equivalent to an extra £39 billion a year.[4]

There can hence be no doubt that wasted potential comes with severe economic penalties. Whether we rake in an extra £140 billion or £39 billion annually, a more socially mobile country would come with greater levels of prosperity all round and significantly more spending power for the treasury. To spell out the significance of modestly increasing economic growth by boosting social mobility, mull over this: during the first wave of the Covid-19 pandemic, the cost of the furlough scheme (from March 2020 to early September 2020) was around £35 billion.[5] Clearly, the economic benefits of boosting social mobility are too good to miss.

A key reason why an increase in social mobility would improve macroeconomic performance is that in more socially mobile societies, the talents of all people are better utilised. As Oxera explains, this tends to improve productivity, as workers' skills and abilities will be better matched to the jobs they do.[6]

By facilitating a stronger economy, an increase in social mobility could genuinely help us to build back better. By tearing down the barriers that stand in people's way, societies would not only be putting right a social injustice, they would also be getting the most out of their labour force, reaping the economic rewards in the process.

A number of levers could be pulled in order to achieve a more prosperous and socially mobile economy. Levelling up educational outcomes – which was the topic of the last chapter – will support people from all backgrounds to access pathways to fulfilling careers. But even if equality of excellence is achieved, everyone would still need to be equally able to navigate the landscape of career opportunities. For that reason, it is essential that all young people enjoy an outstanding careers education.

In a society with true equality of opportunity, no one's aspirations or career successes would be constrained by their socioeconomic background. And they wouldn't be constrained by their gender or ethnicity either. Everybody would be equally informed about the landscape of career opportunities available to them. This would require an in-depth knowledge of what particular jobs involve, how well they pay, how one can reach these jobs, and where particular jobs might lead to subsequently. Everyone would have equally high levels of support in choosing a career that was right for them. And every single person could be confident that if they put their mind to it – and their back into it – they could achieve anything: no ambition would be off limits.

But we don't yet live in a society with true equality of opportunity. In the UK, your understanding of the options available to you in the future and your beliefs about what you can achieve are unfairly influenced by your socioeconomic circumstances. In the words of Nick Chambers, CEO of Education and Employers:

> Too often young people's ambitions are narrowed by an innate sense of what people from their background should aspire to and what's out of reach.[7]

All young people should be made aware of the whole landscape of opportunities that awaits them. They should also be given the skills and confidence to navigate this landscape and arrive at the right destination for them. But many young people are subtly steered towards a particular subset of opportunities based on incomplete information and a saddening sense of where people like them fit in.[8] The ultimate aim of careers education should therefore be to open up opportunity, allowing young people to explore the wide range of career options available, understand the routes into these careers, gain in confidence, develop key skills, and work towards the qualifications required to grasp these opportunities.

It should be emphasised that 'what's right for them' doesn't necessarily mean the best-paying job possible, or even the most prestigious; it means the career that they'll find most fulfilling. And 'most fulfilling' will be different for everyone. Achieving social mobility does not require individuals from disadvantaged backgrounds to be pressured into becoming management consultants or investment bankers regardless of whether they consider these professions to be fulfilling and in line with their personal preferences. But it does require working towards a situation where people from all backgrounds who are – or might be – interested in these professions have the same chance of entering either of them. So overall we should expect to observe a rise in the number of people from less privileged backgrounds entering the most prestigious and well-paid professions – including banking and consulting.

To realise this goal, careers education needs to be phenomenal for everyone. Fortunately, there exists a respected framework that has established a set of clear benchmarks that careers guidance should meet. The Gatsby Benchmarks were first put forward in a 2013 report, entitled *Good Career Guidance*.[9] In 2017, the Department for Education made the benchmarks a central plank of their Careers Strategy, arguing that 'The Gatsby Benchmarks have set world-class standards, and now we want every school and college to use them to develop and improve their careers provision'.[10] In preparing for the report, Sir John Holman (a professor of science education), led a project to review best practice in careers guidance both internationally and in a number of independent schools. Having established the practices and provisions that work well, eight benchmarks were put forward so that schools in England could replicate the best standards of careers guidance.

The motivation for establishing these benchmarks, and launching the review that spawned them, is made clear in Lord Sainsbury's foreword to the report. Here, Lord Sainsbury notes that a situation in which too many students had been 'kept in the dark' had been 'allowed to persist' for too long. Ofsted had also highlighted similar concerns about the previous state of careers guidance.[11]

The Gatsby Benchmarks have become recognised as the gold standard in careers education and are proving instrumental in raising the bar across the UK. The first benchmark, 'A stable careers programme' requires that schools actually have a careers education plan, and that they are strategically driving towards positive outcomes for students. The careers programme must have the 'explicit backing' of senior leadership, and its development and implementation should be led by a properly trained member of staff. Without this benchmark, students could be left with nothing more than a piecemeal scattering of experiences accompanied by uncoordinated snippets of advice. Naturally, this would cause most harm to those who were not receiving additional support from family and their wider networks.

'Learning from career and labour market information' (Benchmark 2) is essential for allowing students to understand the opportunities that are available to them with enough clarity to decide which option is right for them.

'Addressing the needs of each pupil' (Benchmark 3) is vitally important. All students have different aspirations, and the advice and support they receive should be tailored so that everyone can realise their aspirations. Benchmark 3 also stipulates that people's aspirations should not be unfairly influenced by their circumstances or ground down by low expectations.

Schools should not see careers education as a stand-alone programme, but should be strengthening careers education by 'linking curriculum learning to careers' (Benchmark 4). To gain a deep understanding of what particular careers entail, and of what happens on a day-to-day basis in a particular job, students should experience 'encounters with employers and employees' (Benchmark 5) and 'experiences of workplaces'(Benchmark 6). And to gain a meaningful understanding of the routes leading into these careers, learners should have 'encounters with further and higher education' (Benchmark 7). Finally, every student should receive 'personal guidance' (Benchmark 8) so that they can get bespoke advice from a qualified careers adviser.

The benchmarks have been well received. 94% of careers guidance leaders are reported to believe that these standards have improved careers education.[12] Acting in unison, the Gatsby benchmarks will help all young people to navigate their own path to a career that's right for them. The challenge then is ensuring that all schools invariably meet each benchmark in full. But to date, the average number of benchmarks met in full per school is three out of a potential eight. The benchmark met in full most often by schools, Benchmark 8 (personal guidance), is still only achieved by 57% of schools. And the benchmark that is met in full least often, Benchmark 3 (addressing the needs of each pupil), is only achieved in full by 20% of schools.[13] This is particularly disappointing. All young people should be given, in full, the skills and information to navigate the landscape of opportunity, allowing them to forge a path that meets their aspirations and allows them to lead the life they want to lead – rather than the life that some ethereal roll of the dice has laid out for them. But as it stands, only a fifth of schools manage to provide a careers programme that actually tailors advice and support to the needs of individual students. Moving forward, technology can be utilised to meet the Gatsby Benchmarks to the highest degree, thereby making an outstanding careers education the norm for everyone. Let's see how.

Virtual internships

As Benchmark 6 makes clear, it is important that all young people get to experience what a variety of workplaces actually look and feel like. One reason this is particularly pressing from a social mobility standpoint is that many young people – particularly those who are not from privileged backgrounds – may have few opportunities to visit and explore numerous workplaces and hence gain direct experience of a wide range of career options. As the saying goes, you can't be what you can't see.[14] If you have a limited understanding of what the job of a banker, a management consultant, a lawyer, a graphic designer, a pharmacologist or an architect entails, these professions may seem like mere nebulous possibilities rather than concrete aspirations. Actually visiting a large volume and variety of workplaces, however, allows young people to internalise what a range of prospective careers might involve. Furthermore, as Benchmark 6 stipulates, through these experiences young people can begin to develop key professional skills, understand professional norms and expand their professional networks.

It is therefore necessary that young people gain ample experience of different workplaces. It should also be clear that the more opportunities young people have to visit workplaces the better, as visiting more workplaces increases your chances of finding inspiration. But giving students opportunities to explore a wide range of workplaces is incredibly difficult due to inevitable limitations on students', schools' and employers' time, and on employers' capacities to offer workplace visits.

By purposefully utilising technology, however, aspiring professionals may be able to have their cake and eat it. If aspiring professionals could explore the inner workings of a wide variety of professional workplaces virtually, before deciding which workplaces they'd like to experience in person, then they could gain both the breadth and depth of insight needed to make informed, aspirational decisions about their futures. The underlying principle here is that in order to give students the best chance of finding a pathway that they could passionately pursue, it is important for them to explore as many potential career options as possible – and I mean actually explore, just reading an info page does not cut it. If a person only ever has experience of one or two careers or job types, the risk of them settling for a 'fairly good but by no means perfect' option – or of not finding inspiration at all, and hence being left aimless and despondent – is increased significantly. But there are real barriers to providing students with opportunities of enough workplace experiences to explore a cross section of potential options. They wouldn't have the time to complete a work-shadowing experience every single week (particularly if you add up the time it takes to organise these experiences, travel to and from workplaces, and then add that on to the time actually spent shadowing). They may well have time to complete a new virtual internship each week, however. Employers couldn't accommodate an unlimited number of students, but virtual programmes would only be limited by bandwidth. And virtual internships also have the added bonus of allowing people from anywhere in the country (or the world) to participate, and not just those who live locally. While this doesn't address the fact that opportunities are not equally distributed throughout the country, if someone were inspired by a virtual internship, they may be more likely to pursue an in-person internship, even if this means temporary relocation (providing the internship paid properly; more on this point later).

Virtual internships are not a distant prospect. Students can already complete a pioneering virtual internship programme with top law firm Linklaters, which allows them to 'interact with virtual clients and colleagues in a way that replicates the day-to-day work of Linklaters'.[15]

This virtual internship is a prime example of how advanced technologies can upgrade social mobility. The programme harnesses an innovative virtual reality platform[16] in order to give students from all backgrounds the opportunity to experience what it would be like to work for a leading law firm. As explained on Linklaters' website:

> We know that a simple lack of awareness of what life is like at firms like Linklaters is often one of the biggest barriers preventing otherwise strong candidates from applying to join. We hope this new virtual platform will give students a taste of what it's really like to experience the day to day work of a City firm and inspire them to find out more. The programme links our investment in innovation and agility with our commitment to providing applicants from any background, university or degree with an insight into our work and the tangible skills they need to succeed at Linklaters.[17]

After initially opening up the virtual internship to 'students from any university, background or degree',[18] Linklaters has since extended this opportunity to sixth-form students as well.[19] If innovations similar to this groundbreaking virtual internship were widely utilised by employers across all major industries, then aspiring professionals (from students at school to graduate-scheme applicants) could potentially gain valuable insights into a plethora of workplaces and career opportunities, and they could build some key skills along the way.

Virtual internships could also be an especially powerful in situations in which it would be too dangerous for people to get first hand experience.[20] With VR, users are already exploring what it would be like to drive tanks in the Army.[21] The technology is there for them to gain a tangible sense of the work done by firefighters and surgeons.[22] Indeed, VR is already set to play a key role in pilots' training, allowing them to practise and develop essential skills in a low-risk environment.[23] Similar innovations could potentially be used to give people from all backgrounds a visceral sense of what it would be like to fly a plane for a living.

There are three underlying reasons why virtual internships will help to boost social mobility. Firstly – as has already been noted – individuals get to tangibly explore workplaces in order to make informed decisions about where to get experience in person. If everyone can gain constructive experiences of a wide variety of workplaces, this will diminish the asymmetries of information about careers opportunities that exist between those who are well endowed with social capital and useful networks, and those who aren't. If strategically implemented, these virtual internships will enhance in-person work experiences because people's decisions on where to gain work experience, or which professionals to shadow, will be informed by much richer insights into the types of jobs that interest them most.

Secondly, as I have noted, virtual internships could allow people to develop skills directly, ranging from specific technical skills – such as how to fly a plane – to more general competencies such as sending operationally important emails to clients. Without these innovative, accessible opportunities to develop such skills, those with the best contacts will remain at a considerable advantage.

The third factor is, in my view, the most important: inspiration. Achieving one's aspirations takes character.

You'll almost certainly have to wade through doubt, cope with setbacks, and demonstrate bucketloads of grit and determination. The robustness required is much easier to muster if you are confident that the end goal is worth the effort. That kind of confidence necessitates inspiration. Reading a paragraph about a career is not likely to be sufficiently inspiring. But being immersively shown what it would be like to perform a particular role might well do the trick.

Social platforms

Technology can be a powerful ally in achieving Benchmark 5 as it offers a means of connecting learners to employers and employees on a greater scale than would otherwise have been possible. Take Prospela, a professional networking platform for school and university students, through which students connect with e-mentors who can provide live insights into their working day, give tailored advice and help students to develop personalised career plans.[24] By using Prospela, students from all backgrounds can have valuable interactions with employers/employees on a regular basis. Indeed, 85% of users said the platform gave them 'the most authentic, personalised insight they've had to the world of work so far'.[25] This is particularly exciting from a social mobility standpoint. By enabling students from all backgrounds to develop valuable professional networks,[26] innovations that increase the quality and frequency of interactions with professionals will lead to a level playing field in terms of the advice and support that young people can benefit from.[27]

Technology opens up new possibilities. The number of employers/employees with the capacity to connect with students remotely is larger than the number who have time to travel to a school to meet with students or who are in a position to accommodate young people at their place of work on a regular basis. Extending the pool of employers and employees that young people have access to increases the number of encounters they are likely to have; it also means they can have encounters with a greater variety of people, and that they can be more selective with regards to which employers/employees they interact with.

But the benefits of social media-style platforms for aspiring professionals extend past volume, variety and personalisation of interactions. Learning from the example of LinkedIn, we can see that careers-oriented platforms are not just useful for finding and connecting with potentially useful professionals; they are also a means by which one's work and skills can be acknowledged and developed upon, which in turn can allow individuals to gain recognition and build their brand. Two features of LinkedIn stand out here. Firstly, LinkedIn is not just used as a tool for one-on-one private interactions between professionals: people openly showcase their work and achievements by posting to their entire network. Secondly, on LinkedIn, people develop their professional standing via endorsements from their peers. A former line manager, for instance, might endorse a person's skills in strategic planning, public speaking, management, research etc.

These features add value to LinkedIn as a professional networking platform; they could also add value to dedicated platforms for young, aspiring professionals. Already, a key benefit from interactions with employers and employees is that young people get to develop employability skills and build a network of professionals who can attest to them having these skills. By harnessing features similar to those found in LinkedIn, social media platforms for young aspiring professionals could amplify this benefit significantly. Let's imagine Iqra, aged thirteen, has just led a campaign at her school to raise money for muscular dystrophy. She has exhibited astonishing skills of leadership (in both thought and action), communication, organisation, building strong relationships – the list goes on. She has inspired her peers and her teachers with her clarity of vision; she's impressed people with her confidence and ability to follow through; and she's actually reached the tangible goal of raising £654.20. Wouldn't it be great if she could gain recognition for her exceptional work – recognition that could support her long-term career development? And wouldn't it be a well-deserved bonus if she were supported to develop even further so that she can achieve even more spectacular heights in the near future? Social media platforms for aspiring professionals could make this possible. Iqra, and all other aspiring professionals, could use such a platform to demonstrate their extra-curricular achievements along with the skills they have demonstrated along the way. In response, people within the young person's network of professionals could provide valuable feedback. This would support them to understand their achievements, and it would also ensure they were acutely aware of how they had demonstrated key employability skills and how they could develop these skills further still. Professionals within a person's network could also provide endorsements for efforts that had demonstrated certain skills to a sufficient degree. In turn, this may incentivise aspiring professionals to put more focused effort into developing key employability skills through extra-curricular activities. And let's not forget that a young person armed with an abundance of positive endorsements may well have increased access to work experience opportunities, especially as they will also have a fruitful network of professionals to draw upon.

Labour market information

Benchmark 2 states that 'every pupil, and their parents, should have access to good quality information about future study options and labour market opportunities'. Complementing the deep insights gained from mentors and workplace explorations, labour market information gives aspiring professionals an overview of the employment opportunities available in different industries and regions. Such information tends to be produced by large organisations (such as government departments, employer organisations, or trade unions) who collect and evaluate labour market data.[28] Having processed said data, the resultant information is then packaged into a digestible format so that educators and students can make use of it as part of careers education services.

Let's consider the utility of labour market information (LMI) from the perspective of an aspiring professional. After having completed a thrilling VR work experience programme with a pharmaceutical company and then consulting with an e-mentor who works in the industry, our aspiring professional wants to find out as much as possible about the pharmaceutical industry so that they can chart a course of entry into this profession. At a basic level, they could benefit from rudimentary labour market information by being shown a list of job types within the industry, with related information on salary ranges, qualifications typically required, and areas of the country where these jobs are most prevalent. While this information may be of some use, it is unlikely to add much value over and above the insights they have gained from the wealth of opportunities they have already made use of. For this reason, LMI will need to keep up with innovations elsewhere in careers education. Fortunately, it seems to be doing just that.

The holy grail of LMI would be a 'real-time map' of the labour market, which provided all people (including students and current workers) with fine-tuned, comprehensive and up-to-date insights into the opportunities available, thereby helping them to chart the course that is most likely to lead to a fulfilling career.[29] Nesta has been pioneering progress towards this goal. And they have also identified that key barriers to developing this innovation include the fact that the necessary LMI is 'dispersed', 'often incomplete' and not utilised in a way that is most conducive to positive labour market outcomes.[30] More joined-up data sets and better analytical tools are hence key parts of their solution for realising optimal labour market information. By exploring how innovative data science techniques and 'novel datasets' can be utilised effectively, Nesta is making progress towards next generation LMI technologies that could give beneficiaries detailed yet digestible insights into job opportunities.[31]

A key motivation for developing such tools is to enable workers whose jobs may be at risk to either transition to careers that best match their skill sets, or to identify the most effective training opportunities. As Nesta indicates, these tools may hence be vital for those whose livelihoods have suffered in the economic aftermath of Covid-19; these same tools could also be used to support young people who are setting out on their career journeys.

Advanced LMI may, for instance, be able to give our aspiring professional insights into which careers within the pharmaceutical industry are more likely to expand in the future in terms of the number of jobs available, and which (if any) are likely to contract. Having such a wealth of information at their fingertips will truly empower students and help all young people to make informed decisions about their careers. No longer will sophisticated insights into how to enter particular professions be monopolised by those with the best connections. We should hence eagerly await progress towards the next generation of LMI tools, and look forward to the positive impact they could have on students and workers alike.

Supporting Benchmarks 1, 3 and 8

So far, I have demonstrated that targeted innovations can boost efforts to fulfil Benchmarks 2, 5, and 6. But technology also has a role to play in supporting Benchmarks 1, 3, 7 and 8 (I'll come back to Benchmark 7 in the next chapter).

As a reminder, Benchmark 1 states that 'Every school and college should have an embedded programme of career education and guidance that is known and understood by pupils, parents, teachers, governors and employers.' Benchmark 3: 'Opportunities for advice and support need to be tailored to the needs of each pupil. A school's careers programme should embed equality and diversity considerations throughout.'

And Benchmark 8: 'Every pupil should have opportunities for guidance interviews with a career adviser, who could be internal (a member of school staff) or external, provided they are trained to an appropriate level. These should be available whenever significant study or career choices are being made. They should be expected for all pupils but should be timed to meet their individual needs.'

Technologies should be used to undergird the fulfilment of these benchmarks for two key reasons. Firstly, to coordinate careers programmes effectively, and in a way that responds to students' needs, schools and colleges need to have a clear understanding of the progress students are making along their career journeys. Secondly, to ensure that they are optimally empowered as part of careers education programmes, students should have as much control as possible over the information, resources and services that they access. In short, schools need oversight, learners need ownership.

An effective embedded careers programme should not be a regimented litany of activities, chosen without regard to students' changing needs and aspirations. As students learn more and more about what they might want to do later in life, careers programmes should adapt and respond to these developments. To ensure that such programmes can be inherently flexible so as to tailor support to individual needs, schools need to record and monitor students' progress along their career journey. A school or college should be aware, for instance, of what virtual work experience programmes students are completing so that they can tailor further support for them. A school should be aware of which e-mentorship programmes are most effective and for which groups of students, so that they can signpost students to the most beneficial programmes or resources. To achieve this, schools should use appropriate platforms. These could be styled on information management systems that schools currently use to record information such as students' attainment and attendance. Having oversight of students' experiences of careers support will enable schools to constantly adapt and refine their careers education strategy (as per Benchmark 1) and also ensure that experiences can be increasingly personalised for students (as per Benchmark 3).

Benchmark 3 could also be supported by ensuring that students can take charge of their own nascent-stage professional development. Students should have direct access to advanced LMI, the most exciting virtual internships and the very best e-mentors. And when they attend invaluable careers guidance interviews (Benchmark 8), they should have the option of sharing a record of all the careers-based activities they have engaged with, so that those interviews can be properly tailored to each student's ambitions.

Standing on the shoulders of the giant that is the Gatsby Benchmarks, the purposeful deployment of innovations could ensure that all young people receive a careers education that helps to propel them forward to wherever it is they want to go.

But let's not forget that to fulfil the promise of the Gatsby Benchmarks with aplomb, learners and educational institutions are still heavily reliant on the willing and enthusiastic participation of employers and employees. Virtual internships will need to be co-created with the companies themselves to provide representative experiences. And to sustain a vibrant pool of e-mentors, organisations may need to provide encouragement and inducements to their staff. It is hence appropriate to question whether we can expect companies to take such an active role in this process.

On this point, we must remind ourselves that it is in the interest of individual employers to play a leading role in boosting social mobility. The best person for the job may not come from the most affluent household. According to the Social Mobility and Child Poverty Commission – which is now the Social Mobility Commission – employers' efforts to drive social mobility and develop an inclusive workforce can achieve 'increased productivity and drive', 'improved performance' and 'improved staff loyalty and engagement'.[32] The Association of Certified Chartered Accountants has also emphasised the importance of social mobility, stating that 'promoting social mobility is not just the right thing to do, it also helps assemble a workforce better suited to today's interconnected and complex global economy.'[33]

We can hence be hopeful that companies will, in vast numbers, rise to the challenge and roll up their sleeves to support innovative practices in careers education. Indeed, as soon as a critical mass of socially responsible companies start to offer virtual internships and/or programmes whereby staff serve as e-mentors on social media platforms, it will be in the interest of their competitors to follow suit. They wouldn't want to let their rivals dominate talent pipelines after all. The fact that many companies are, as we've seen, already offering innovative opportunities for prospective employees to learn more about them boosts confidence that such a critical mass can be reached.

Making recruitment fairer

As well as working to fuel young people's aspirations towards the beginning of the talent pipeline, employers should also be expected to ensure that recruitment is fair so that people from all backgrounds can thrive in the labour market – it is in their own interest, after all. Technologies can be instrumental in achieving this goal. Rare, a company that provides an innovative contextual recruitment system, is achieving great successes as part of their mission to enable those from disadvantaged backgrounds to successfully pursue 'rewarding careers', and 'to make their talents and drive accessible' to the organisations to which they could add significant value.[34] By analysing data points such as 'postcode, examination grades, whether the applicant was looked after, or first in their immediate household to go to university',[35] Rare gives context to a person's achievements.

As Raphael Mokades, Rare's founder and Managing Director, has explained, the principle at work here is that a person's academic achievements do not necessarily give a clear picture of their true potential because the circumstances in which these achievements were made differs from person to person:

> Three As at A-level for a candidate from Eton tells recruiters less about an individual's potential and resilience than three As for a candidate from an inner-city comprehensive school in special measures.[36]

Numerous high-profile employers utilise Rare's system,[37] which enables them to harness the best talent within the labour market and 'identify candidates with the greatest potential'.[38] And Rare is making a difference, with 61% more candidates from disadvantaged backgrounds being hired when the contextual recruitment system is used.[39]

This example hits upon a more fundamental principle: by transforming data into valuable insights, technology will enable people's talents to be properly recognised and utilised. (Contextual admissions for universities is another area in which this principle manifests itself – more on this in the next chapter). Looking at the case of contextual recruitment specifically, innovations are already allowing employers to make recruitment decisions that are both fairer and more appropriate in terms of employers' own needs. We should reflect on the fact that a key selling point of systems that provide context to a person's achievements is that they help companies recruit the best people. The system is unearthing talent that might otherwise have remained hidden. Missing out on these sources of talent could be bad for businesses because a) there are opportunity costs to not employing people with the potential to be the most productive and highly performing professionals in an organisation, and b) rivals could exploit this talent pool and gain a competitive advantage. This dynamic is promising. While acknowledging the fact that many employers are genuinely committed to social justice issues (including equality of opportunity) and are doing great work in this regard, if it is systematically in employers' own interests to do their utmost to recruit talented people from all backgrounds, then this should increase our confidence that levels of social mobility could actively be driven upwards across the board, and in a sustainable way.

The next hurdle

Access to fulfilling careers could be made significantly more inclusive by enhancing careers education in schools and supporting employers to unearth hidden talents. Unfortunately, however, there are further hurdles to clear. Even when individuals from less privileged backgrounds gain access to fulfilling careers – including the most elite and prestigious professions – they tend to make less progress in their careers than those from more affluent backgrounds.[40] Levelling up education and careers guidance, and initiating smarter recruitment practices, may hence achieve greater inclusivity among the more junior professional ranks, but these levers may be powerless to address disparities in who rises highest.

In their book, *The Class Ceiling: Why it Pays to be Privileged*, Sam Friedman and Daniel Laurison examine this problem forensically. They show that within the most elite professions, individuals who come from working-class backgrounds earn on average £6,4000 per annum less than individuals from privileged backgrounds. For elite professionals who come from families where neither parent earned, the gap increases to £10,000 per annum.

As Friedman and Laurison emphasise, these disparities cannot be understood purely in terms of merit. Gaps in earnings still exist even when degree classification achieved and type of university attended are accounted for. First-class graduates who come from privileged backgrounds earn on average £7,000 per annum more than first-class graduates who come from less privileged backgrounds. For Oxbridge graduates, the annual premium for being from a privileged background is £5,000.

Together, these findings are profoundly disheartening. They lay bare that even if a young person achieves academically and makes effective decisions about their career, their life chances could still be unfairly influenced by their socioeconomic background. But Friedman and Laurison go beyond documenting the headline problems. Their work is tremendously valuable in that it explains how these patterns arise and reveals why a person's background can have such a strong impact on their career trajectories. They discuss a number of factors that contribute to disparities in career progression rates, including the practice of informal sponsorships, which those from more privileged backgrounds tend to benefit from most; the fact that those from more advantaged backgrounds are often seen as a better cultural fit within top professions and the matter of people from less privileged backgrounds knowingly eschewing opportunities for progression towards more prestigious roles at a greater rate than those from other backgrounds.

The latter factor, which Friedman and Laurison term 'self-elimination', is particularly noteworthy, as it reveals a darker side of social mobility. Acknowledging that self-elimination could be construed as some people just being less ambitious and determined, Friedman and Laurison argue that a key reason people from less privileged backgrounds self-eliminate at a greater rate is that they anticipate that success will be accompanied by emotional damages, and therefore act to avoid situations in which they would feel like an 'imposter' – 'othered', 'uncomfortable' and 'out of place'.[41] This echoes findings presented in Mike Savage's *Social Class in the 21st Century*.[42] The book relays findings from both the *Great British Class Survey* and a series of follow-up interviews. In the book, Savage demonstrates the 'profound emotional imprint' that social mobility can have on the upwardly mobile, noting that many upwardly mobile people who were interviewed felt 'torn between two worlds'. Sam Friedman has drawn upon similar insights elsewhere to argue that social mobility may not be 'straightforwardly "beneficial"' because of the 'considerable psychological price' that people often have to pay for economic gains.[43]

As Friedman and Laurison show, if moving up is so often equated with moving out, leaving part of your world behind, and entering a new, somewhat alien one, then social mobility might not be an invariably pleasant experience after all. In *The Class Ceiling*, Friedman and Laurison hence claim that 'despite the prevailing political rhetoric, upward social mobility is not the unequivocally positive force often assumed in wider society.' While I maintain that there are no credible arguments for why a person's life chances should be unfairly influenced by their socioeconomic circumstances at birth, I sincerely sympathise with the point that social mobility can put people in the intolerable position of feeling they are abandoning their communities, rejecting their roots, and becoming more distanced from family and friends.[44] Just because life chances shouldn't be unfairly influenced by one's backgrounds, doesn't mean that people should be forced to renounce their background.

In my view, the solution to this problem is to strive with ever more vigour towards greater levels of social mobility. If people from all socioeconomic backgrounds had an equal chance of entering and succeeding in the highest-paid and/or most prestigious professions, then very soon these professions would become genuinely representative of society as a whole. As a result, nobody would need to feel out of place due to their upbringing.

But although this might be the right approach in the long term, there is the problem of circularity to contend with in the short term. For those whose career progression is being hampered by feelings of anxiety and a sense that they don't belong,[45] promises of a distant vista where inclusivity reigns supreme may not be a credible solution to their problem. If they don't progress, then an opportunity is lost to make senior roles incrementally more inclusive, rendering said vista even more distant.

And if making small steps proves difficult, making the giant leap to optimum inclusivity will be far harder still. We shouldn't lose hope, however. Achieving ambitious goals is never easier, but that doesn't mean we should not strive towards greater levels of social mobility. Parallels can be drawn here with the words of John F Kennedy:

> We choose to go to the moon in this decade and do the other things, not because they are easy, but because they are hard, because that goal will serve to organise and measure the best of our energies and skills, because that challenge is one that we are willing to

accept, one we are unwilling to postpone, and one which we intend to win...[46]

Turning our attention back to the core problem, as Friedman and Laurison show, even when people from less advantaged backgrounds secure jobs in the professions – having achieved the same grades at the same universities as their new-found colleagues – they are still likely to be less successful in their careers on average. This means that even if educational inequalities are addressed, the playing field will remain unlevel. Friedman and Laurison's research gives us strong insights into the nature of the problem, and the golden thread linking the mechanisms (noted above) that lead to disparate progress rates can be summed up in one word: bias. Friedman and Laurison's work demonstrates that preconceived notions of what potential, talent and professionalism look like are heavily biased towards the characteristics of those from more privileged backgrounds. In turn, this can make those from other backgrounds feel as though they don't fit in.

It is important to reflect that this potential for bias will have varying impacts on different people in different contexts. As Friedman and Laurison show, some people may even be unconvinced that these entrenched biases exist at all, or they may feel that they are easy enough to circumvent so as not to be inhibitive. After all, many people who have entered the professions from less affluent backgrounds have managed to fit in and make progress in their careers.[47]

The fact remains, however, that, as Friedman and Laurison have shown, there is a 16% pay gap that cannot be fully explained by merit-based factors such as educational attainment and experience alone. Friedman and Laurison cogently make the case that biased notions of ability and suitability do contribute to the pay gap between people from different backgrounds. They also indicate that this factor may contribute to pay gaps between people from different genders and ethnicities: note that the average black female professional from a working-class background earns £20,000 less a year than her white, male counterpart from privileged beginnings.[48]

In order to address these biases, the capacity to draw insights from data will be key. Advanced technologies may be highly effective in this respect, but significant progress could also be made via less high-tech solutions. As Friedman and Laurison urge, organisations should 'critically interrogate' their own biases. They encourage organisations to 'measure and monitor' the relative progression rates of employees from different backgrounds, in order to understand and counteract any previously unidentified biases. They also note that while many organisations are already doing this proficiently: others are not. The priority, therefore, should be ensuring that all employers collect and analyse the basic data that is needed to assess their own biases. According to Friedman and Laurison, this data should include information on whether employees had been eligible for free school meals, the occupations that their parents were in and whether they were the first in their family to go to university. The application of more sophisticated data collection and processing methods could become normalised at a later date, but the priority has to be collecting and making use of this kind of data in the first place.

CHAPTER 6

FURTHER ROLES FOR TECHNOLOGY

Early years

As things stand, our life chances are unfairly influenced by our circumstances at birth. And while the results of this initial lottery are not quite powerful enough to determine all of our successes in life, in many cases one's starting point can provide a pretty strong indication of what's to come.

The Education Policy Institute has shown that by the time they start school, children who are eligible for free school meals are already 4.3 months behind those from more affluent families.[1] As lamentable as this is, the following finding, reported by the Department for Education, is perhaps even more unsettling:

> By the age of three, more disadvantaged children are – on average – already almost a full year and a half behind their more affluent peers in their early language development.[2]

To make matters worse, the evidence also suggests that once gaps emerge, they often grow wider. The Education Policy Institute has shown that the aforementioned gap of 4.3 months during early years widens to 9.4 months at the end of primary school and then widens further still to 18.4 months at key stage 4 with the most disadvantaged falling 23.4 months behind at this point.[3]

Recalling the thought experiment from Chapter 1, spectators from behind the veil of ignorance will be able to see that this state of affairs will not do. If a person were to enter the world blindly, they would have no way of predicting what circumstances they would be born into. But as soon as they step into this world, predicting what's to come becomes much easier. If someone is born into a less privileged socioeconomic group, there's a strong chance their developmental opportunities in early years will be worse than those enjoyed by their more advantaged peers. Their literacy, numeracy and general development is likely to lag behind, culminating in them being less able to benefit from full-time education when they get to that age. As things stand, if you start near the bottom, there is a significant chance that's where you'll stay.

So what can be done to change things? Well, first of all let's be clear that there is not going to be a tech-based miracle solution. A suboptimal early-years education system coupled with entrenched socioeconomic injustices contribute to the gaps observed in early years development. As we will explore momentarily, early years educational provision desperately needs an upgrade. Furthermore, as the Education Policy Institute observes in their report *Key Drivers of the Disadvantage Gap*,[4] the impacts of growing up in a disadvantaged household itself hinders development. It should be obvious that poorer-quality housing, limited access to basic amenities and the stress that naturally accompanies precarious economic circumstances cannot be good for childhood development. These circumstances mean that disadvantaged families face additional challenges to supporting their children's personal development (more on these pivotal factors in Chapter 9).

Bridging the gulf entirely may therefore require sweeping reforms: there is unlikely to be a silicon bullet solution.[5] That said, there are clear indications that technology could lend a helping hand to narrow the divides in early years development between different socioeconomic groups.

Sesame Street provides a good omen here. A meta-analysis of studies into the impact of this much-loved TV show, conducted by Marie-Louise Mares and Zhongdang Pan, found the programme to be 'an enduring example of a scalable and effective early childhood educational intervention'.[6] Meanwhile, in their work, *Early Childhood Education by Television: Lessons from Sesame Street,* Melissa Kearney and Philip Levine demonstrated that young people who were able to access *Sesame Street* were '1.5 to 2 percentage points more likely to be at the grade level appropriate for their age'.[7] Their study relied on the fact that when *Sesame Street* was first launched in the USA in 1969, not all counties could access the programme. By comparing outcomes for similar children between the counties that did have access to *Sesame Street* and the counties that didn't, they established a significant positive correlation between access to *Sesame Street* and positive early years development. They also showed that *Sesame Street* had a particularly positive impact on young people who grew up in the most disadvantaged counties.[8]

The programme took its endeavours to educate and entertain very seriously. High-quality, engaging learning material was at the heart of each episode; content was grounded in the science of early childhood development,[9] and *Sesame Street* was particularly focused on supporting the development of young people from more deprived backgrounds.[10] *Sesame Street*'s success provides hope that inspirational content can begin to combat inequalities in childhood development. There is also hope, therefore, that with more advanced technologies to draw upon, the developmental gulf can be bridged to an even greater extent. A resource that we should be especially excited about comes, in part, from the makers of *Sesame Street* themselves.

Sesame Workshop and IBM have teamed up to create 'the next generation of individualised learning tools'.[11] (By the way, IBM's innovative software, Watson, also provides the technology behind Ada,[12] the digital assistant tool used at Bolton College which we met in Chapter 4; and it is the computer programme that defeated the all-time top scorers of *Jeopardy,*[13] discussed in Chapter 2). Working in collaboration, the two organisations have developed a platform that can support the advancement of young people's vocabularies through individualised learning.[14] As leading figures at IBM and Sesame Workshop explain, this platform will 'enable software developers, researchers, publishers, educational toy companies, and educators to create individualized learning experiences'.[15] By combining Watson's artificial intelligence with Sesame Workshop's proven ability to create learning material that is both highly stimulating and effective,[16] this innovation could rival, or hopefully even surpass, the positive impacts that *Sesame Street* has had on early years development. Given that the original vintage had a significant equitable impact – improving outcomes for the most disadvantaged by the greatest amount – there are grounds for optimism that IBM and *Sesame Street*'s co-created platform (and other innovations like it) may have a resoundingly positive impact on social mobility by raising literacy levels in an equitable way.

As well as supporting learners directly, technologies can also be used to observe and evaluate young people's development, and hence provide recommendations for educators – or parents, guardians and other carers – on how best to support a particular child. Oyalabs, for instance, has developed a tool that can build a child's 'unique developmental profile' to give carers a 'personalised activity plan' for their child.[17] A device is placed in a child's room or play area and, by monitoring verbal interactions, can build up a picture of the child's 'language environment', measuring the number of words that have been spoken to them, the number of 'engaged, back-and-forth exchanges' they've had with people, and even the quality of these interactions.[18] Based on the child's individual needs, carers are given recommendations on how to support the child and aid their development.[19]

As they become more and more widespread, a range of innovative resources will aid the developments of young children to a significant extent. But remember, to comprehensively address inequalities between children from different socioeconomic groups, those from the least privileged backgrounds would need to extract the greatest benefits from these innovations. An issue that must be addressed directly, therefore, is the potential for variation in average levels of parental engagement between different socioeconomic groups. According to the Sutton Trust, for instance, whereas 78% of three-year-olds from the highest income families are read to every day, this is true of only 45% of three-year-olds from the lowest-income families.[20] Fortunately, technologies can be utilised to address disparities in parental engagement head-on.

EasyPeasy is an early-years programme that has been supported by the Parental Engagement Fund, an initiative established by the Sutton Trust and the Esmée Fairbairn Foundation with the aim of '[increasing] attainment for disadvantaged children in the early years through the development of more effective parental engagement'.[21] As explained in a report evaluating the programme:

> EasyPeasy is a programme that aims to improve child development by increasing positive parent-child interaction through play at home. It uses the mobile phone as a channel to reach parents and carers, giving them inspiration and ideas for real-world games and activities.[22]

EasyPeasy also links parents/guardians to each other and to educators/educational institutions, thereby creating a strong, supporting community around each learner.[23] EasyPeasy's value lies in its ability to provide high-quality content that expands parents' repertoire of activities and games to play with their children, and in its capacity to bring people and organisations together to share best practice and achieve a coordinated approach to developing each individual child. The app was found to have a positive impact on parents' 'sense of control' and on children's self-regulation, which has been shown to be an important indicator of a child's school-readiness.[24] Tools such as these are hence likely to play a pivotal role in equalising the effectiveness of parental support for early years development.

Elsewhere, there are positive indications that e-books could be beneficial to children's development. As explained in the paper, *Use of Electronic Storybooks to Promote Print Awareness in Preschoolers who are Living in Poverty*, authored by academics at the University of North Carolina Wilmington and Michigan State University, e-books can help to build children's vocabularies and comprehension skills. E-books add value not as gimmicks, but because they can employ specialist features that support children's literacy.[25] As the aforementioned paper explains, they can support children to become familiar with the fact that words are read from left to right, for instance, by tracking the print as they read. The report also highlighted the fact that some e-books contain in-built dictionaries to support children with the meaning of individual words, and others employ sophisticated print-referencing methods, which help readers make sense of the overall meaning of what they are reading. As another string to their bow, e-books could potentially be more inclusive than their predecessors. The Dyslexia Association notes that e-books often allow users to change background colours, font types, the magnification of words and the spacing between lines.[26] Looking forward, e-books could also become a vital tool for garnering information about how children's reading skills are developing by unearthing patterns in the words they struggle to decode. This information could be fed to parents, guardians or teachers to provide tailored interventions.

I have no doubt that purposefully applied digital innovations will play a meaningful role in levelling the playing field of early years development. Digital tools can support learners directly through personalised delivery of high-quality content and more broadly by enabling interactive and pedagogically robust experiences; they can also help children indirectly by furnishing educators and guardians with increased insights into children's needs, and by increasing the confidence and coordination of their carers' support. We should be buoyed by these prospects, but we should not forget that analogue approaches in the form of system-wide reforms will need to play an even bigger role than tactical innovations in order to achieve a universally high standard of early years development.

A critical problem that needs to be overcome is that early years care is often more about occupation than education. Providing affordable childcare for working families is an economic imperative, a necessary service for keeping society ticking over. But alas, in efforts to maximise the availability of affordable childcare, the equally important goal of providing effective educational development opportunities has been compromised. Quantity has taken priority over quality. Those who desperately need a high standard of early years education – one that prevents them from falling behind – lose out most from this settlement.[27]

There are two possible routes forward. Shift the balance to prioritising quality of education over quantity of affordable provision, which could hit working families' finances hard (and even disincentivise work altogether). Or maintain current quantities of provision and invest in a much-needed boost in quality. In the spirit of equality of excellence, the latter option is wholly favourable. So what's at the heart of the currently underwhelming performance of early years provision? None other than a lack of investment in skilled, qualified teachers.

The Sutton Trust, in their *Mobility Manifesto 2019*, prescribed the following policy solution, which hits the nail on the head:

> Priority should be given to ensuring more early years teachers gain Qualified Teacher Status, with the increase in pay, conditions and status this would entail. The aim should be to have a qualified teacher in every setting. The government should also invest in improving qualifications for all practitioners in the sector.[28]

Great teachers make all the difference. McKinsey has even noted that having an effective early-years teacher can significantly boost the chances of a student completing higher education.[29] As such, any effort to reform early years provision must start with renewed efforts to ensure all of society's youngest children have access to fantastic teachers. And to aid these teachers in setting these children off on inspiring, engaging, life-chance-boosting learning journeys, they should have access to the best resources possible. The same technologies that could assist pupils at home – from platforms that provide personalised learning experiences to tools that help to analyse children's development – will undoubtedly have a role to play in formal early years settings too. Like humble servants, technologies will be ready to be called upon to play their roles dutifully and with purpose.

Promoting fair access to higher education

Despite efforts to rectify the situation, unequal access to higher education remains an acute pain point for social mobility. One aspect of this pain point that has been particularly well documented is the disparities in admissions between state-educated and privately educated students: the latter group being more than twice as likely to gain a place at a Russell Group university and seven times more likely to secure a place at Oxford or Cambridge.[30] These statistics take into account disparities in the rates at which students apply to these institutions. But a similar story is told when we look at just the students who do submit applications. If you were to apply to a Russell Group university, you would be significantly more likely to be accepted if you were privately educated (71% chance of acceptance) than if you were state-educated (44%).[31] Looking more broadly, Teach First has reported that young people from more advantaged backgrounds are 5.9 times more likely to attend the most selective universities and that only 24% of pupils who are eligible for free school meals progress to university, compared to 42% of pupils who aren't eligible.[32]

The status quo is not good enough: change is needed, now. Technology can play a key role in bringing about positive changes in access to higher education, and can also be used to widen access to other aspirational routes after full-time education, such as apprenticeships. Here the role for technology closely mirrors that which it played in the context of careers education and recruitment (which was discussed in Chapter 5). Just as technology can allow students to make informed decisions about the pathways they could take towards fulfilling careers, innovations can be harnessed to ensure that young people can make informed decisions regarding which paths to take immediately after full-time education. And in the same way that technologies can be used to ensure talented applicants are not overlooked during recruitment processes, digital tools will also ensure that universities admit the best possible students – something which, as we'll see, can't always be ascertained through grades alone.

But it's important to be clear from the outset that the most important lever for ensuring that all socioeconomic groups are proportionally represented at universities is the equalisation of attainment. On this note, the following finding from the Office for Students is particularly enlightening:

> When disadvantaged students achieve the same levels of attainment as their advantaged peers at age 16, they are almost equally likely to go to higher education. However, only one-third of disadvantaged students get the GCSE grades associated with higher education entry, compared to two-thirds of their advantaged peers.[33]

Increasing the quality of the education a person receives on a daily basis should hence be the priority. But as we have discussed this point in great depth already, we'll move swiftly on to other aspects of the solution.

Helping students realise their aspirations

While addressing asymmetries in academic attainment must be the priority, efforts to untangle the myths and misconceptions around higher education – those which can dampen a student's motivation – are also desperately needed. Indeed, there are currently cases where parity in attainment is being achieved but where equality in access to universities is not. This can be seen in admissions to Oxbridge. Among students who achieve A*s in their GCSEs (grade 8/9 in new money), there has been a 3.6 percentage point gap in admissions between students who were eligible for free school meals on the one hand and those who weren't eligible on the other.[34] As Teach First has argued, 'It is not simply a question of getting the right grades – [students] also need to make informed decisions about their futures'.[35] As such, measures to ensure that people have the information they need to convert their academic successes – and forge forward along an aspirational path after compulsory education – have an important role to play in achieving fairer admissions.

As the example of Oxbridge admissions shows, there is evidence that among the highest-achieving pupils, those from the least privileged backgrounds are disproportionately making less aspirational decisions than those who occupy the rungs above. While Oxford and Cambridge will never be for everyone, we should not be content with the fact that high-attaining pupils from less privileged socioeconomic backgrounds eschew the opportunity to attend these prestigious institutions at a greater rate than their more affluent peers.

The problem is not isolated to highly selective universities, however. Polling from the Sutton Trust has shown that 67% of students among the least affluent groups have strongly considered attending university, which is sixteen percentage points lower than the 83% of students from the most affluent group who said the same.[36] There are even alarm bells warning that the least affluent groups are less likely to make use of opportunities provided by apprenticeship programmes –which have previously been heralded as a new dawn for social mobility – with 28% of people from the most advantaged areas taking up higher-level apprenticeships, compared to 13% of people from the least advantaged areas.[37]

Let me be crystal clear, the problem that needs addressing here is not that young people from wealthier backgrounds are inherently more aspirational than those who are less privileged. The problem is that, at a macroscopic level, there are significant differences between the decisions the two groups make about their futures. Blaming a lack of ambition is in effect saying that less affluent young people are poorer decision-makers whose judgements are clouded by timidity. The alternative explanation is that those from less affluent backgrounds are making decisions based on incomplete information, with their judgements naturally skewed by their environments. Loic Menzies, CEO and founder of the Centre for Education and Youth, has argued against the notion that disadvantaged young people are inherently less aspirational. Rather than assuming that low aspirations are the root cause of some people's lack of success and therefore focusing efforts on raising their aspirations, Menzies argues that educators should move to a model where sufficiently high aspirations are assumed and efforts are pivoted towards supporting students to crystallise and reach these aspirations.[38] In essence, we should be supporting students to realise, not raise, their aspirations.[39]

The need to inform and support students' aspirations is something schools and colleges, and universities themselves, are very much aware of. For schools and colleges, Gatsby Benchmark 7 promotes frequent encounters with further and higher-education institutions, i.e., trips to universities, opportunities to attend lectures, visits from academics/ university students.[40] For universities, to charge students the maximum amount in fees, they are obliged to have formal processes in place to widen participation.[41] Furthermore, an ecosystem of social enterprises already exists to support schools, colleges and universities with these endeavours. Technologies can be used to supplement and amplify these efforts, enabling young people to realise their aspirations to a greater extent.

There are, of course, strong parallels between careers education and efforts to broaden access to higher education. We have already seen in Chapter 5 that technologies can be used to illuminate the landscape of opportunity, bringing light to the shadowy valleys which might otherwise have been left unexplored. This applies as much to careers as it does to higher-education/apprenticeship opportunities. In both contexts, technologies can facilitate a greater level of personalisation in the support young people have access to. With regards to widening access, research indicates that more tailored approaches to nurturing a specific individual's aspirations are more effective than approaches that are 'generically inspirational'.[42]

Social media-style platforms could therefore be used to connect school-age students with university ambassadors whose experiences and interests resonate with their own. Intelligent matching, or even just features that enable filtering for the most appropriate mentor, could ensure that these experiences were anything but generic. Imagine being able to pick a mentor from the shelf who had similar goals and life experiences to you: that may well be preferable to being paired with someone at a local university who happens to be studying a subject that you're interested in.

We've also seen previously that employers are beginning to virtually open their doors to prospective recruits through virtual internships and VR exploration experiences. Universities, and also apprenticeship providers (who are themselves employers after all) could make use of similar tools to engage with prospective students virtually. Students could potentially attend a virtual lecture at a world-class university, and then take part in a virtual internship with a leading multinational company – both on the same weeknight evening. If inspiration struck, they should then be given further opportunities for in-person encounters at these institutions; digital resources should never supplant in-person experiences.

Ensuring people from all backgrounds have an equally demystified understanding of future educational opportunities could make a significant difference to access rates between people from different socioeconomic groups. We should not be leaving innovative solutions that can make gains here on the bench. That said, efforts that focus on realising aspirations can only ever be the support act to approaches that equalise attainment. Then again, absolute equality of attainment may not, in fact, be necessary.

Promoting access through contextual admissions

In most cases, the gaps that exist between different socioeconomic groups tend to get wider over time, leading to ever greater disadvantages for those less privileged. But graduation results tell a different story. Based on comparisons between degree classifications achieved by students educated privately and those educated in the state sector, students from less privileged backgrounds actually start to make up considerable ground on their more advantaged peers throughout higher education. All things being equal, students who went to state schools are more likely to achieve a first-class degree or a 2.1 than students who were privately educated. To illustrate, among students who achieved the equivalent of eight A grades at GCSE, 73% of state-educated graduates went on to achieve a 2.1 or above compared to 69% of privately educated graduates; and among students who achieved the equivalent of 8 B grades, 52% of state-educated graduates went on to achieve a 2.1 or above compared to 43% of privately educated graduates.[43]

This trend opens the door to another possible way to bridge the gulf in access to higher education: contextual admissions, i.e., the practice of making students different offers, based on factors such as their socioeconomic backgrounds. The Sutton Trust has shown that widespread use of this practice could potentially increase the number of disadvantaged students (defined as those eligible for free school meals) at highly selective universities by 50%,[44] demonstrating that this mechanism could be a powerful lever for equalising opportunity. But before diving straight in and mainstreaming this practice, questions need to be addressed around how to ensure contextual admissions are both fair and valid.

To an extent, concerns over the fairness of contextual admissions are justified. Offering students from disadvantaged backgrounds a university place based on significantly lower grades than those required of more advantaged students may increase the diversity and inclusivity of universities, but this could also result in inappropriate penalties for more advantaged pupils who may be equally deserving of a place. Imagine a relatively privileged student was made an offer to attend a prestigious university on the condition that they achieved A*AA in their A levels, but that they missed out narrowly when they achieved a highly respectable AAA. How would they feel if someone elsewhere had been successfully admitted with EEE? Clearly there is a point at which the fairness of contextual admissions becomes questionable.[45] It should also be clear, however, that in many cases the use of differentiated offers is without doubt fair and valid. Would you bat an eyelid if an individual from a highly disadvantaged background were admitted to the same university course as per the above example, having achieved three As at A-level, or AAB? I certainly wouldn't.

The best way to conceptualise the line that demarcates fair and valid from unfair and invalid contextual admissions is to consider that attained qualifications don't just provide a record of your achievements to date, they also serve as an indicator of your future potential.[46] With regards to the former of these functionalities, qualifications and grades represent a universal standard of achievement. Two students who achieve ABB in the same A-level subjects have the same level of attainment: simple. But what is much more complex is the question of whether that means these students are equally likely, for instance, to succeed in achieving a 2.1 or above in their degrees. To answer this question, we need to move away from describing prior attainment and towards predicting future attainment.[47]

As we have already seen, if one of these students was educated at a state school and the other at a private school, there is evidence to back up the prediction that the former would outperform the latter at university, despite the two having attained the same A level grades. The sweet spot for contextual recruitment would therefore be the point at which both students would be likely to achieve at the same level in their degrees.[48] The Higher Education Funding Council for England, for instance, has reported evidence to suggest that a state-educated male student who attained BBB is just as likely to achieve a 2.1 or above as a privately education male student who attained ABB (a similar dynamic is observed with female students too).[49] This might therefore justify an approach whereby state-educated students were made offers conditional on slightly lower grades, not because the bar should be lowered for them arbitrarily but because they would have demonstrated equivalent aptitude to privately educated students. Of course, for the most deprived students, equivalent aptitude may be demonstrated by significantly lower grades – BCC perhaps. Remember, they have overcome far greater barriers then their more affluent peers. Contextual admissions hence present a legitimate avenue for ameliorating the social mobility pain point of university admissions. As long as the bar is kept universally high in terms of admitted students' aptitudes, then charges of unfairness and invalidity can be decisively laid to rest.

The majority of highly selective universities already use contextual admissions to some extent.[50] The categories of data relevant for making contextual admissions decisions include data pertaining to the school an individual attends (note that past higher-education participation rates vary wildly between schools), the area in which the person lives, whether the individual has participated in formal access schemes and data pertaining directly to the individual themselves (e.g., whether they have been eligible for free school meals).[51] Of these categories, individual-level data is considered to be the most effective for making valid contextual admissions decisions.[52] That said, this category of data is underutilised within the general admissions process.[53] Innovations are needed in how this type of data is collected, processed and shared so that universities can make better informed contextual decisions. The Centre for Social Mobility at the University of Exeter has urged that organisations such as the Department for Education should be seen as 'crucial partners' in improving access to reliable data sets.[54]

Yet again we are seeing the impact of the fundamental aptitude of technology to collect, process, share and most of all draw meaningful insights from data. As we have seen previously, such insights can be used to aid an individual's development, but these insights can also be used to better recognise the extent to which individuals have already developed, thereby further diminishing unfair advantages currently held by the most privileged.

Reimagining assessment

As well as enhancing teaching and learning, it is anticipated that technology could revolutionise how learners are assessed. As it has been argued, such a transformation could address a number of critical shortcomings in the current assessment paradigm. Pertinently, it is also possible that a paradigm shift in how learners are assessed could have positive implications for social mobility.

In their authoritative report, *Preparing for a Renaissance in Assessment*,[55] Dr Peter Hill and Sir Michael Barber interrogate the desired goals of assessments and put forward a strategic vision of how, through innovative practices, these goals can be achieved to a greater extent than at present. They emphasise that assessments serve the formal purposes of 'certification, selection and accountability', as well as the formative purpose of improving teaching and learning. From this premise they pinpoint shortcomings within the current assessment paradigm relative to these goals and also offer practical, innovative solutions.

They highlight that current assessments rely heavily on grades and single scores, which obscures a true understanding of the learning outcomes that a student has achieved. This practice could be replaced, they suggest, with 'more immediate, detailed and meaningful reporting' achieved by using e-portfolios, for instance. They also emphasise the following problem:

> Tests and examinations [are] dominated by questions assessing low-level cognitive processes and [are] failing to capture such valued outcomes as practical, laboratory and field work, speaking and listening, higher order cognitive processes and a range of inter – and intra-personal competences (so-called 'twenty-first century skills').

They hence suggest that new platforms could be designed to assess a broader range of competencies and attributes.

Hill and Barber also argue that innovative approaches could result in assessment systems that can capture students' abilities in a more holistic way, that are less easily gamed and that can support teaching and learning as part of a more constructive, formative cycle. Potential innovations include adaptive tests, which can assess a broader range of students' competencies in a shorter amount of time, and 'sophisticated online intelligent learning systems' that can assess pupils over long periods of time and provide feedback to teachers and learners.

Hill and Barber are by no means alone in advocating for a renaissance in assessment. Professor Rose Luckin, an authority on artificial intelligence in education, has emphasised that AI could revolutionise how learners are assessed. Luckin argues that the status quo is stressful for students, and represents an inefficient use of teachers' and learners' time. That said, she also acknowledges that plausible and comprehensive alternatives have not been available, at least until recently. Luckin notes, for instance, that coursework has become less prevalent due to concerns around the authenticity of students' work.[56]

AI provides a 'best of both worlds' solution, marrying the objectivity of examinations with the potential of less structured assessments to capture a more genuine reflection of a learners' skills, knowledge and abilities. As Professor Luckin notes, AI-based assessments could even provide a representation of skills such as collaboration and persistence and attributes such as confidence and motivation.[57]

To envisage what an AI-driven assessment paradigm might look like, and how it would differ dramatically from the status quo, imagine (or remember) the experience of passing your driving test. After weeks, months or years of becoming an increasingly safer, more competent driver, you are strapped in and about to start your driving test, the objective of which is to assess whether you are indeed safe and competent enough to drive independently. While the driving test has been an unpleasant experience for many people over the years, few would advocate for the test to be scrapped. After all, there needs to be some way of ensuring that only proficient drivers are allowed on the road. But what if there were another way to systematically test a driver's proficiency? What if, as you were learning and developing as a driver, your progress was being monitored on an ongoing basis, perhaps by some software installed in the car. What if this software could track your development as a driver, assessing you against key competencies? And what if this software could identify the point at which you had become a sufficiently safe, accomplished driver, and therefore award you with your licence? Instead of you learning to drive, then judging that you might be ready to take your test, and then proving yourself right or wrong by taking the test, here you are being assessed as you learn as part of a seamless, integrated process.

This is the underlying principle of how AI-driven assessments would work. Instead of learning and then being assessed, you would be assessed as you learn.[58] As Professor Luckin explains, the assessment process would take place over an extended period of time, potentially a full school year or even longer.[59] Such a shift could pose a number of benefits.[60] Firstly, assessing learners in an ongoing, cumulative manner would provide a more accurate picture of their abilities. Secondly, this approach could also provide a broader picture of students' abilities because not all skills are best tested through a written assessment taken under exam conditions; on this point, it has been suggested that AI assessments could even be built into activities such as games or collaborative projects.[61] Thirdly, with this approach, formative assessment achieves equal status with summative assessment. The information that AI systems would be collating on students' learning would not solely be used for the purpose of awarding credentials, it would also be used to support students on an ongoing basis.[62] As discussed in Chapter 4, and as Hill and Barber themselves emphasise, formative assessment has been demonstrated to be one of the most powerful levers for improving learning outcomes. AI could do more than formally assess learning, it could actually drive the learning process itself.[63]

Building upon the points discussed in Chapter 4, we can start to put together a picture of how a transition to AI-driven assessments could occur. If learners come to routinely use adaptive learning platforms for personalised learning (both in school and out), and further AI-based resources are used to empower teachers with insights into learning (such as the example given of the formative assessment of collaborative learning projects, which didn't involve students directly using a device), then we may be approaching a point where there is sufficient data to provide a robust representation of a learner's knowledge, skills and attributes.

In Sir Anthony Seldon's *The Fourth Education Revolution*,[64] he puts forward a positive vision of where this could lead. Anticipating that the 'Holy Grail' of learning in the fourth education revolution would be for learners to benefit from AI-enabled personalised learning for some portion of each lesson, he notes that 'the wealth of data produced by students week on week will equally allow AI to produce fully tracked CVs on each student's performance'. He argues that AI-based assessments of learning will provide information that is 'more comprehensive and forensic' than that provided by exam grades and test scores, and hence resoundingly predicts the welcomed death of 'the all-conquering cumulative exam'. But if the current assessment paradigm does come to meet its maker, what impact might its passing have on social mobility?

It is difficult to predict the exact impact that such a transition would have on social mobility, though we can make a number of considered conjectures. It could, for instance, be argued that moving away from high-stakes summative assessments, and towards AI-driven continuous assessment, would benefit disadvantaged students because they are less likely to benefit from some exam-technique premium, a set of distinct skills that sit over and above mastery of the curriculum. Any potential asymmetries here could be explained by disparities in access to private tutoring,[65] parental support or the quality/ focus of teaching and learning more generally. This claim definitely has some credibility when you consider the case of the 11+, for which, as I have already noted, parents often invest handsomely in private tuition. As Professor Rose Luckin has argued, a selection system based around continuous assessments would leave no opportunity for wealthy families to marshal their resources in preparation for one-off exams.[66] But elsewhere there is insufficient evidence to suggest that more advantaged learners systematically benefit from an exam-technique premium for every single exam. We cannot be sure that the gap in GCSE or A-level attainment can be explained, either in part or in full, by one group of students being better at passing exams per se than their peers. A more likely explanation is that they benefit from a higher standard of teaching and learning; an advantage they could easily maintain within a new assessment paradigm. We cannot, therefore, predict with any certainty that a renaissance in assessment will have a direct and immediate impact on attainment gaps. That said, it is possible that grammar school intakes would become more socially diverse.

There is, however, an alternative argument for why a renaissance in assessments could boost social mobility, which I find altogether a lot more convincing. The intensive focus on preparing students for exams has been strongly linked with a narrowing of the curriculum, which, it has been argued, has had an adverse effect on the rounded development of young people – particularly the most disadvantaged. By facilitating a broader, richer curriculum, an AI-based assessment paradigm has the potential to allow people from all backgrounds to gain the full spectrum of skills needed to flourish.[67]

There is more to education than passing exams. While making the case for a 'renewed focus' on a richer curriculum, Amanda Spielman (Ofsted Chief Inspector) argued that, in the past, school inspections had placed 'too much weight on test and exam results' which had 'increased the pressure on school leaders, teachers and pupils alike to deliver test scores above all else.' She also lamented that curricula had been narrowing in schools, noting that at Key Stage 2, lessons were too heavily focused on maths and English, and that in secondary schools practices that centred around preparing students for GCSEs had led to many learners dropping subjects such as art, music or history as early as twelve or thirteen years of age.[68]

Vignettes of an even darker side of this tunnel-visioned focus on passing exams have arisen. *Tes* (formerly referred to as the *Times Educational Supplement*) has reported that a fifth of schools have sent six and seven-year-olds home with practice SATs papers to complete; and they also reported that eleven-year-olds were already working towards GCSEs, despite not having to take the exams for five years.[69]

Elsewhere, academics at the University of Kansas and the University of Alabama have argued explicitly that fixating on exam results tends to 'distort' the purposes of education, particularly through 'curriculum narrowing',[70] which causes subjects that are not assessed to become sidelined.[71]

I should note at this stage that I am strongly of the view that we should not dismiss the importance of supporting young people to pass their exams. After all, high levels of academic attainment are an essential component of equality of excellence. The fundamental point, however, is that the academic core of the curriculum on which students are so intensively assessed is necessary but not sufficient.[72] Yes, all students from all backgrounds should be supported to excel in subjects such as maths, English, science and languages. Qualifications and competencies in these subjects can open doors and set students up for the future. But there are significant opportunity costs to apportioning too much of learners' time to studying these subjects at the expense of others. Research has indicated that the narrowing of the curriculum and an intensive focus on exams is preventing students from developing the skills and competencies needed to succeed in later life.[73]

Employers and universities themselves have argued that the existing exams system doesn't fully equip students with the complete range of skills they'll need to flourish in life, after they leave school.[74] And in *The Fourth Education Revolution*, Seldon explicitly notes that the narrowing of the curriculum brought about by the desire to raise exam results has resulted in a reduction in less privileged people's life chances, rather than a boost.[75] Systematically sidelining opportunities to develop a wide range of desirable skills has a particularly adverse impact on young people from disadvantaged backgrounds, as these people tend to have less opportunity to develop these skills outside of school.[76] A narrow curriculum may hence be a contributing factor to social immobility, a point which Lee Elliot Major (co-author of *Social Mobility and its Enemies*, and the UK's first Professor of Social Mobility) has raised, asserting that 'art, sport and other aspects are just as important' for social mobility.[77]

An AI-based assessment paradigm could address this problem. And while it may not be the only solution, it could well be a powerful one. In such a paradigm, all or most aspects of learning would be assessed on an ongoing basis, meaning that schools would not be compelled to prioritise either the aspects of the curriculum that learners would be tested on or the tests that were deemed more important. In the AI assessment paradigm, all aspects of learning matter. In this paradigm, schools would be better placed to support students to develop those desirable skills and attributes which are often overlooked: communication, collaboration, even grit and resilience – all skills that AI is anticipated to be able to measure.[78] As Sir Anthony Seldon has emphasised, 'AI opens up an education offering a much broader enrichment for all'.[79] This could be tremendously advantageous from a social mobility perspective. The shift from high-stakes exams to AI-based continuous assessment has the potential to facilitate equality of excellence not just in terms of academic attainment, but also in terms of the broader set of skills needed to flourish in life.

CHAPTER 7

LIFELONG LEARNING AND THE DIGITAL ECONOMY

As the name implies, lifelong learning refers to opportunities for personal and/or professional development that are available throughout all stages of a person's life. Typically, this portion of the education sector has not been a priority for governments, who have instead focused resources on education for young people. This approach may have been appropriate in the past, but it is rapidly becoming untenable. Grappling with the economic impacts of Covid-19 and the likely acceleration of automation,[1] governments are now having to give increased attention to lifelong learning. Before the pandemic, it was projected that as many as 30% of jobs could be at risk of automation by the mid-2030s.[2] A worse fate may now be in store. A career for life is unlikely to be an option for many workers of the near future. It may hence become necessary for people to intensively upskill and retrain throughout their lives and as a result, demand for lifelong learning is likely to soar. Advanced technologies are likely to play a pivotal role in meeting this demand as well as contributing to it.[3]

Due to the ominous prospect of disrupted labour markets, the interplay between lifelong learning and social mobility is particularly complex. As stated in a report co-authored by the Boston Consulting Group and the Sutton Trust, 'Without concerted effort, social mobility could deteriorate further due to trends shaping the future of work.'[4] There are hence justifiable concerns that the factors that will provide the impetus for lifelong learning could actually harm social mobility. But that does not mean we shouldn't welcome an expansion in learning and development opportunities for people of all ages. As we will see momentarily, an inclusive lifelong-learning sector can achieve the dual benefits of equitably increasing opportunity for adults while retroactively reshaping the landscape of opportunity for young people. As they have done in the past, innovations will continue to facilitate flexible, affordable, high-quality, effective and fulfilling lifelong learning opportunities. Fuelled by an innovative and inclusive lifelong-learning sector, not only will societies be much better placed to withstand the tempestuous times ahead, they will also be better equipped to boost social mobility.

Towards an innovative, inclusive lifelong-learning sector

The Open University (OU) provides a shining example of how purposeful innovations can be utilised to increase the availability and inclusivity of lifelong learning. The OU's founding purpose was to give those who'd missed out on higher education as young adults the chance to attend a world-class university in later life.[5] The University's model has therefore always allowed students to learn flexibly and over a longer period of time, meaning that commitments can be balanced with having a job and a family.

Throughout the years, innovation has been key to making this model work. To some, the technologies that were initially utilised – VHS for instance[6] – may seem outdated now, but they were certainly used to great effect. Today, the OU's students have access to more advanced digital solutions such as online forums for peer discussions and online tutorial sessions, which continue to fulfil the promise of premium lifelong learning.[7]

The Open University is just one part of the oasis that is the lifelong-learning sector. Community education centres, further education colleges, training providers, private education companies, and employers who train and develop their existing workforces in-house are some other elements of this 'rich tapestry'.[8] The modes of learning deployed by these different institutions vary from largely face-to-face learning to entirely online models. Among the most ubiquitous innovations facilitating online learning opportunities are massive open online courses (MOOCs). With MOOCs, learners access content online – usually via a dedicated platform – which may vary from pre-recorded lectures to more bitesize forms of learning material. MOOC platforms often include features that enable collaboration and peer-to-peer support, such as forums. In fact, leveraging opportunities for interactions among large groups of learners was a key motivation for developing the trailblazing MOOC *Connectivism and Connectivity Knowledge*, which was launched in 2008 and accessed by over 2,000 learners online.[9] Since then, MOOCs have become a staple of the lifelong-learning sector.

Moving forward, MOOCs are likely to make increasing use of the smorgasbord of educational technologies we have explored so far. VR/AR is likely to be used where appropriate to enhance engagement and to effectively teach certain concepts and skills. It may be normal for adaptive technologies, including chatbots,[10] to be integrated into these courses. And it has even been predicted that artificial intelligence will be utilised in the form of lifelong-learning partners.[11] These learning partners could serve as the missing link between compulsory and lifelong-learning systems. As the authors of *Intelligence Unleashed* explain, 'There are no technical barriers to the development of learning companions that can accompany and support individual learners throughout their studies – in and beyond school'.[12]

As powerful as these innovations may be, the lifelong-learning sector should not exist solely in the ether. The rich tapestry of institutions referred to above must continue to provide the human touch. But by introducing technologies into the mix, the capacity of the lifelong-learning sector as a whole can increase substantially, leading to an abundance of affordable, high-quality provision and a richer plurality of opportunities. For adults, the advantages to be gained from an inclusive lifelong-learning sector are self-evident, but adults are not the only group of learners that stand to benefit. By increasing – and also pluralising – the developmental opportunities that are available throughout a person's life, opportunities might also become more evenly distributed among young people.

To understand, at a fundamental level, how institutions such as the OU improve the landscape of opportunity, we can invoke the concepts of 'bottlenecks' and 'opportunity pluralism', developed by Joseph Fishkin. To illustrate these ideas, think about the most common route towards achieving a degree. In the UK, most undergraduates enter university as young adults, having recently completed further education (where they were most likely awarded A-levels, BTECs or the International Baccalaureate). This could be described as a bottleneck because, without the existence of the OU or similar such organisations, if this particular trajectory was not a good fit for you (perhaps because of your circumstances, or even just your preferences) you would be unlikely to gain a degree, which would close off further opportunities to you.

For young people considering their options, the OU effectively diverts some of the traffic away from this bottleneck; it creates a new route via which individuals can gain a degree, meaning that the decisions people make at the age of seventeen or eighteen needn't have such high stakes. Apprenticeships, which provide an additional route towards fulfilling careers, are another example of how opportunities are being pluralised and bottlenecks are being addressed. As the number and quality of apprenticeships on offer increases, studying for a degree may cease to be the primary well-defined path to tread.

Central to Fishkin's argument for focusing on pluralising opportunity and addressing bottlenecks, is the idea that equality of opportunity is wholly unattainable, and that the pluralisation of opportunity is both preferable and more realistic. He argues, for instance, that the role of the family will always lead to opportunities being distributed unequally, due to the variation in resources that families have at their disposal.[13] As my arguments throughout this book have hopefully made clear, I happen to disagree with Fishkin here. And while I share his enthusiasm for the pluralisation of opportunity, I do not see this as an alternative or competing endeavour to the equalisation of opportunity.

The pluralisation of opportunity complements and reinforces equality of opportunity. The litmus test for whether equality of opportunity has been achieved is whether or not a person's life chances are unfairly influenced by their circumstances at birth. If circumstances wield a significant influence over a person's life chances, then the impact of a person's talents, efforts and aspirations are intolerably diminished. Equality of opportunity is therefore as much about empowerment as it is about fairness. Pluralising opportunity also empowers individuals. The Open University empowers people by providing an alternative means of gaining a degree. More generally, an inclusive lifelong-learning sector could potentially reduce the importance of gaining a degree (more on this point momentarily), thereby empowering those for whom university is not the best option.

As well as driving towards the common goal of empowerment, the pluralisation of opportunity can, in practice, aid the equalisation of opportunity directly. Fundamentally, this is because bottlenecks in the opportunity landscape have a tendency to privilege the privileged; removing these bottlenecks by pluralising opportunity hence tends to distribute opportunity more fairly.

Bottlenecks can inhibit social mobility because they serve as tripping hazards, which disproportionately affect the less advantaged; bullseyes, i.e., targets at which those with sufficient means can aim their resources; and strongholds that come to be systematically dominated by the elites.[14] To demonstrate, a situation where students can only gain a degree as a young adult presents a tripping hazard because those whose circumstances make it less easy to attend/reach university are likely to trip up at disproportionate rates. The 11+ clearly acts as a bullseye as seen by the fact that parents from wealthier families often invest substantial resources in tutoring and coaching. The widely acknowledged 'well-trodden path' from private schools, to Oxbridge, to roles in the heart of government or well-paying jobs in the City provides an example of a stronghold. In this case, an established route to success has (to some extent) come to be dominated by the elites to the exclusion of others. Do note, however, that the proportion of students at Oxbridge who were state-educated is nearing 70%.[15] This is well below what one would ideally expect given that 93% of people attend state schools, but also much higher than some people realise. I mention this because perceptions of elitism and exclusivity can often lead to self-fulfilling prophecies – something we should avoid at all costs.

Through the pluralisation of opportunity, lifelong learning can circumvent tripping hazards, remove bullseyes and dismantle strongholds. As previously noted, the OU has enabled huge numbers of adults to access university for the first time, thereby compensating for the tripping hazard presented by the erstwhile 'one-shot' model for getting a degree. Lifelong learning more broadly could also be an effective means of overcoming strongholds. Universities and even apprenticeships are disproportionately accessed by people from more advantaged backgrounds. These are pathways of proven efficacy: those who attain degrees or complete apprenticeships are likely to dominate the most sought-after jobs. For sure, many people do immediately become full-time employees after leaving compulsory education and then 'rise to the top'. But the rate of ascent via this route isn't comparable to the fast lane that higher education provides. With greater availability of lifelong learning, there may be less of an expectation that incoming employees should be the finished product in terms of their educational development. This may result in a greater emphasis being placed on training and upskilling on an ongoing basis, meaning that graduates and those who have completed apprenticeships are less able to saturate higher-end jobs because there will be more and more pathways open to others to reach the same destinations.

In short, lifelong learning will naturally pluralise opportunity, and this in turn will help to equalise opportunity as strongholds are vanquished and tripping hazards avoided. When opportunities are perishable – as they will inevitably be without inclusive lifelong learning – the privileged are at a distinct advantage as they are better placed to get their fill ahead of others. But when opportunities endure throughout a person's life, everyone has the chance to indulge.

In principle, the combined forces of equality and plurality of opportunity should synergistically enhance people's life chances. That said, I do have concerns that in practice a tunnel-visioned focus on the plurality of opportunity could undermine equality of opportunity. While new pathways could open up and threaten existing strongholds, these same pathways could instead be used to justify diverting efforts away from supporting people from all backgrounds to succeed via the established routes. We should be wary, for instance, of any new qualifications/initiatives that were targeted at people from less advantaged backgrounds; and we should always ask ourselves, 'If it's not good enough for the most privileged, why should it be good enough for everyone else?'

It should be emphasised, however, that this issue does not represent an unavoidable tension between pluralising opportunity and equalising it. Indeed, funnelling one group of people down a newly created pathway is not actually in the spirit of pluralising opportunity at all as nobody would genuinely be empowered with a greater degree of choice over how they progressed and developed. Similarly, this issue should not dampen enthusiasm for an inclusive lifelong-learning sector. As long as we remain zealously committed to equalising opportunity at all stages of a person's life, then there is no credible threat that the pluralisation of opportunity will cannibalise equality of opportunity.

This brings us to another essential ingredient of inclusive lifelong learning: ensuring that the benefits of lifelong learning are felt equally by adults of all socioeconomic groups. Achieving this goal will not be without its challenges. This is made clear by the fact that the Learning and Work Institute has found that more disadvantaged, less well-educated adults are significantly under-represented among adult learners.[16] There is hence cause for concern that lifelong-learning opportunities will be primarily seized by well-educated adults, which could exacerbate pre-existing inequalities. Looking specifically at MOOCs, concerns have been raised that those most in need of additional educational support are least likely to take up and complete courses.[17] That said, it should be recognised that MOOCS are not inherently biased towards more advantaged groups. In particular, where MOOCs and the broader educational programmes in which they are embedded are specifically designed to support less advantaged groups, there have been notable successes – especially where these learning opportunities are designed in collaboration with the people they aim to benefit.[18] Moving forward, all institutions delivering lifelong learning should ensure that their provision is appropriate for a wide range of individuals from different contexts.

The issue of inequality of uptake also points to the importance of getting things right the first time around. If people from all backgrounds have equally positive experiences of education from day one, and if they are all fully cultivated to become voracious lifelong learners, then the oasis of opportunity offered by lifelong learning might genuinely be available to all in practice, not just in theory.

An inclusive lifelong-learning sector, which confers a greater plurality of opportunity and improves equality of opportunity, is the holy grail. The pluralisation of opportunity brought about by a burgeoning lifelong-learning sector will empower individuals with more choice over how they progress throughout their life, while also overcoming the bottlenecks that have a tendency to cause most damage to the life chances of the less privileged. Meanwhile, equalising opportunity from day one will ensure that the exciting new developmental routes are inclusive to people from all backgrounds. As the Open University has proven, innovation can be instrumental to achieving this objective.

In its own right, an inclusive, innovative lifelong-learning sector is a goal worth striving towards. That said, will realising its promises be enough to counteract the impacts of automation? Will the innovations that enhance lifelong learning be able to keep pace with those that disrupt the labour market?

Technology is driving formidable economic changes, and there is no guarantee these will be inherently good for social mobility. According to PWC, 30% of jobs risk being automated by the mid-2030s.[19] McKinsey has shown that right now for six in every ten jobs, 30% of the tasks performed could be automated by adapting technologies that already exist.[20] Meanwhile, Nesta has predicted that over six million people in the UK are likely to see their jobs disappear or at least 'change radically' by 2030.[21] And these prognoses were made before the economic quakes caused by the Covid-19 pandemic, which is likely to accelerate the adoption of automating technologies. Within this brave new world, the dizzying pace of change could mean that workers will constantly need to upskill or retrain just to tread water.

It is hence incumbent on societies to facilitate retraining and upskilling opportunities for any worker who may want or need them. Fortunately, innovative digital resources are already being called upon to rise to the challenge of maintaining workers' employability. The Flexible Learning Fund, for instance, is an £11.4 million fund that encourages and supports innovative approaches to learning for working adults.[22] The CareerTech Challenge, a £5.75 million programme launched by Nesta and the Department for Education, is promoting the development of innovative tools that will enable individuals to secure and succeed in fulfilling jobs.[23] The programme aims to support people who do not have a degree and earn less than £35,000 per annum.[24] The CareerTech Challenge is linked to the National Retraining Scheme (NRS), an upcoming public service that will support the economically vulnerable to retrain and hence transition to more secure positions within the labour market. The development of the NRS, which is due to be fully operational in 2022,[25] is a direct acknowledgement of the economic need for widespread lifelong-learning opportunities. The Scheme had its roots in the Industrial Strategy, which was designed to 'improve productivity and build a country that works for everyone'.[26] Attesting to the government's commitment to this project, £100 million was committed just for the design and development of the scheme, and the delivery of the first phase.[27]

As we have already established, technologies are able to enhance the productivity of educational institutions, make highly advanced resources genuinely affordable, improve teaching and learning, extract insights from data (including labour market data) and connect people to each other and to experiences they would not otherwise have had. Given these formidable strengths, I have reasonable confidence that innovations will rise to the challenge of safeguarding people from the perils of automation. Yes, this does mean people will have to devote more time to learning, but it is highly likely that automation will save people at least as much time elsewhere in their lives. People may therefore have the bandwidth to invest their energies in learning and upskilling on an ongoing basis. Thanks to an inclusive, innovative lifelong learning sector, a labour market characterised by constant flux may not be such a harsh environment after all... as long as there is not a net decrease in the demand for labour, that is.

As I noted at the beginning of this chapter, the context of automation results in there being a multifaceted relationship between lifelong learning and social mobility. While in ideal terms, lifelong learning could increase, equalise and pluralise opportunities for people of all ages and from all backgrounds, in reality, an expansion of lifelong-learning may be symptomatic of less favourable labour market conditions, which are more likely to inhibit social mobility than improve it. Yes, there are grounds for optimism that innovations in lifelong learning will counteract the turbulence; but there is no ironclad guarantee of this. That said, we should remember that just as umbrellas don't cause the heavens to open, progressing towards a flourishing lifelong-learning sector will not in and of itself create adverse conditions in the labour market. In its own right, an inclusive, innovative lifelong-learning sector is a goal worth striving towards. So let's do just that.

CHAPTER 8

OVERCOMING THE DIGITAL DIVIDE

We are now armed with a set of innovative solutions that could help to level the playing field; a profoundly exciting prospect. But excitement must be tempered with a sense of caution. If technologies are not utilised in an equitable way then the playing field could actually become more uneven rather than less. This is not an inducement to give up and throw in the towel. Inaction will inevitably lead to a perpetuation of social immobility, to squandered potential, to lives not lived to their fullest. But we need to be aware of the risks that the digital divide presents to social mobility so that we can overcome them.

The underlying reason why these innovations could in fact widen the divides that might otherwise have been closed is that the most privileged could extract the most benefit from technology.

The table below provides a simplified picture of the various ways in which this principle could manifest itself:

Scenario	The less privileged get...	The more privileged get...
1[1]	A technology-centred cheaper education	Enhanced educational provision, where technology is used to augment and supplement the practice of human educators
2	Next to nothing outside of school due to limited access to technology	Access to high-quality technology-based provision outside of school
3[2]	Standard educational provision, without technology being effectively utilised	Enhanced educational provision, where technology is used to augment and supplement the practice of human educators

When I began writing this book it was Scenario 1 that weighed heaviest on my mind. As Professor Rose Luckin has warned, advanced technologies could result in an educational 'apartheid'[3] in which only the most privileged learners will benefit from 'the ideal mix of technology and human interaction', while less privileged learners are left with only 'AI technology and a little human interaction'.[4] As Luckin notes, it's not hard to see how this vision could become reality. Intelligent technologies are cheap (at least compared to highly skilled professionals) and they don't require holidays, sick days, or even a work-life balance.[5] One day some intrepid education minister might decide that Intelligent Tutoring Systems or adaptive learning platforms have proven to be so effective that it would be an outrageous waste of taxpayers' money to continually dole out public funds on a burdensome, bloated teaching profession.[6]

Reforms happen swiftly. Teachers, perhaps already on precarious contracts, are mercilessly dismissed in droves, with only a small minority kept on as glorified 'bouncers'.[7] Unlike children whose families can afford to send them to better-resourced schools, the young people at these bare-bones schools will have limited access – if any – to inspiring role models, they won't benefit from small-group supervision, and they are likely to experience a much narrower curriculum, where personal skills and peer-to-peer interactions are sidelined. And that is only the tip of the iceberg.

In this scenario, the many would get mediocrity on a shoestring while the few enjoyed far more stimulating, rewarding and nurturing uses of technology. Here, the widespread availability of technology has in effect turned upon an already fractured society. Instead of being used to raise standards, technology is primarily being used to cut costs – although in this scenario, opportunity costs caused by a diminished education have gone through the roof. In essence, technology could cause some learners to be tethered to the bottom line.

We should not lose sight of this dystopian possibility. And we must always ensure that the powers that be are put under pressure to not cut corners with people's life chances. Indeed, we should demand of our leaders that they continually raise the bar rather than obsessing over the bottom line. Spending on education is as much an investment as it is an expenditure. Schools that resemble battery farms may well save money in the short term, but by squandering talent and potential, they will cost societies in the long run.

Within the current climate, Scenario 1 is not necessarily the most pressing concern, however. The dividing line between Scenario 1, on the one hand, and 2 and 3 on the other, is that with the former, technology – being abundantly available and of 'sufficiently high quality'(in some people's eyes at least) – poses the risk of eroding or supplanting the invaluable impact of human educators. But with the latter scenarios, technology – remaining a relatively scarce resource – only benefits those who can access it readily. School closures due to Covid-19 have demonstrated the devastating impact that the latter state of affairs can have on social mobility. Indeed, while schools were closed during lockdowns, we saw a version of Scenario 2 play out.

Before the pandemic hit, the scale of the digital divide in the UK had already been acknowledged. It was known, for instance, that approximately one million children did not have sufficient access to a device or even a reliable internet connection at home, and that 11% of young people who did have access to the internet at home still did not have the resources to use a computer with a broadband connection.[8]

As schools closed their gates and home learning became the norm, the tremors arising from this faultline began to be felt. In May 2020 (around two months after school closures began) the Institute for Fiscal Studies announced findings that young people from more affluent families were spending 30% more time learning from home than those from more disadvantaged families.[9] In June, a University College London (UCL) study estimated that around 20% of young people had completed less than an hour's worth of learning a day, and that many of these people had spent no time learning at all.[10] The same study showed that around a fifth of pupils who were eligible for free school meals had 'no access to a computer at home', compared to just seven per cent amongst the whole student population;[11] the study also found that privately educated pupils tended to enjoy significantly greater levels of provision than state-educated pupils.[12]

As a result, any pre-existing progress towards addressing educational inequalities was put in jeopardy; one head teacher even claimed that it would take two years for disadvantaged pupils to catch up.[13] Let's hope that this is an overestimate.

When access to digital hardware and infrastructure became prerequisites for learning, those with minimal access (or none whatsoever) lost out. The unequal distribution of access therefore served to exacerbate educational inequalities and further entrench social immobility. Although innovations in software could equalise opportunity throughout society, this is evidently contingent on people from all backgrounds having access to the hardware and infrastructure needed to actually benefit from said innovations. This is not a theoretical notion. It is a harsh reality. The Covid-19 pandemic has made this clear.

But let's not forget that the inequities observed during the height of the pandemic (which, alas, may be felt for years to come) is not the only way that the digital divide could frustrate progress towards greater levels of social mobility. With Scenario 2, access to hardware serves as a crutch, enabling some learners to stumble on while others fall behind. Meanwhile, with Scenario 3 the danger is that more advantaged learners will accelerate into the distance because the most advanced technologies are being purposefully utilised on their behalf, leaving the rest to cruise along without these enhancements. There is a credible risk that it will be the best-resourced schools that are better placed to adopt advanced technologies. Private schools, for instance, may be in a better position than state schools to invest in the infrastructure needed to benefit from innovations such as VR-based virtual internships and adaptive learning platforms. Standards could be driven up for these schools while they stagnate for others.

Although the problems experienced in Scenarios 2 and 3 are distinct, both predicaments are united by a common solution: equalising access to hardware and infrastructure. This is no pipe dream. Societies can and must secure digital inclusivity as a fundamental right for their citizens.

Before Covid-19, 87% of schools in Estonia were already utilising innovative solutions. Estonia's impressive digital strategy has even been credited with supporting their ascent to the top of the 2018 PISA table among European countries. When home learning was initiated, learners and educators were hence well placed to rise to the challenge.[14] In China, to enable online home learning while schools were closed, major telecom companies were marshalled to increase internet access across the country, particularly in areas of greatest need.[15] Elsewhere, Kenyan authorities partnered with Alphabet Inc. and Telkom Kenya as part of a scheme where high-altitude balloons carrying

4G signals were used to increase internet access, and hence support online learning.[16] Closer to home, in the UK, the Academies Enterprise Trust (AET) bought 9,000 laptops to give to learners who were eligible for free school meals.[17]

These examples should raise hopes that digital inclusivity is achievable. But we can look elsewhere to see that, fortunately, a global pandemic is not required to catalyse decisive action. Before the pandemic, trailblazing schools were already guaranteeing their pupils access to devices for use inside and outside of school. At The Streetly Academy, for instance, students use chromebooks as part of their learning, which they can either buy at a subsidised rate or borrow from the school at no cost.[18] Pioneers such as The Streetly Academy realised that investments in inclusive access to hardware are necessary for extracting the dividends on offer from innovative software. To achieve equality of excellence at scale, the entire school system should follow suit. And in some countries this has already happened.

In 2007 the government of Uruguay established Plan Ceibal, the remit of which was to equalise the opportunities provided by new digital technologies. To fulfil this aim Plan Ceibal ensured that all children in Uruguay had both their own device and free access to the internet.[19] As a result, in Uruguay, universal access to tech-based learning became the norm. Moreover, Uruguay's students don't just have access to hardware and infrastructure, they also have effective software for learning too. The Mathematics Adaptive Platform (the Spanish acronym for which is PAM) tailors the delivery of maths content from the national curriculum to each student.[20] In particular, PAM provides personalised feedback to students based on their individual needs.[21] The evidence indicates that the platform is having a positive and equitable impact. A 2019 study showed that PAM increases students' maths scores, but perhaps more importantly, the study also showed that the less privileged a student is, the more they benefit.[22] This is unlikely to have been the case if being less privileged meant you did not have adequate access to a device and a sufficiently good internet connection.

When the pandemic struck, Uruguay's education system (and the students themselves) benefited from the wealth of technological resources that were already in use.[23] Having previously closed the digital divide to a significant extent, the benefits of online learning were not distributed anywhere near as unequally in Uruguay as in other countries. This provides grounds for optimism that in the near future, the benefits of advanced educational technologies can be felt equally by all learners, provided that decisive measures have already been taken to close the digital divide.

The first takeaway from this discussion is that because there are underlying inequalities in access to the hardware, connectivity and infrastructure, the benefits of the most advanced technologies may not be spread evenly. Moreover, because such access is so often correlated with socioeconomic circumstances, the innovations discussed in this book could actually exacerbate social immobility. The second takeaway is that we can overcome the risk of this happening. The digital divide could well act as a stumbling block as we strive towards a more socially mobile society, but this divide is not inevitable; it can and must be addressed head-on.

CHAPTER 9

WHERE TECHNOLOGY IS NOT THE ANSWER

The golden thread running through this book is that technology can break many of the shackles binding a person's life chances to their socioeconomic background. If people from more privileged backgrounds tend to go to better-performing schools, then they will be able to get ahead. If developmental opportunities outside of formal education are prohibitively expensive, then only those with the necessary means can use these channels to get further ahead still. And if those from wealthier families tend to be better endowed with the knowledge and networks that are vital to navigating the labour market, then they will be better placed to convert their hard-earned skills into tangible economic returns.

As we have seen, by equitably enhancing the productivity and effectiveness of educational institutions, by making educational services cheaper and by expanding people's networks and horizons, technology can unshackle those who are not from an affluent background. This will enable all people to enjoy a wealth of opportunities that have traditionally been dominated by the privileged. Fundamentally, this means that technology can circumvent the influence of financial means in many cases: it is harder for the wealthy to hoard opportunities[1] if they are both affordable and in abundance.

But technology cannot circumvent all the privileges that accompany wealth. In this chapter, I'll outline a number of drivers of social immobility that cannot be solved by technology. Sometimes money matters, and, as such, money itself is needed to break a number of the shackles that hold so many people back.[2]

Some opportunities such as private tuition and private schooling come with a direct cost at the point of use. This can be addressed by driving down the cost of provision, or driving up standards in the state-education sector. In other cases there are indirect costs associated with opportunities, meaning that these opportunities are not always genuinely accessible. Unpaid internships are a prime example of how aspiring professionals often incur such indirect costs as they strive towards their goals. According to the Sutton Trust, unpaid internships inhibit many young people from 'low and moderate-income backgrounds' from entering desirable professions such as fashion, journalism and politics.[3] Looking at the numbers, it is not hard to see why this is the case. Completing an unpaid internship is expensive. The minimum cost of completing a month-long internship is £1,019 in London and £827 in Manchester,[4] which helps to explain why 39% of people who had been offered an internship declined the offer due to financial considerations.[5]

As you might expect, there are gaps in the rates at which people from different backgrounds complete unpaid internships, with 29% of the more advantaged completing them compared to 23% of those from less advantaged backgrounds.[6] The latter group are locked out of this developmental pathway to a greater extent than the former.[7] And even when those from less affluent backgrounds do complete unpaid internships, they are less likely to be able to devote the same amount of bandwidth to their internships because they often have no choice but to take on a separate part-time job to keep them afloat while working full-time for nothing.[8]

Of course, internships themselves are not the problem. They provide important opportunities for people to develop professionally, explore their talents and interests, and make progress in their careers. But to increase access to these high-quality opportunities, the indirect costs associated with them must be addressed head-on.[9]

One proscription from the Sutton Trust, which I wholeheartedly endorse, is for all employers to pay interns at least the national minimum wage where internships last for longer than four weeks (with the national living wage being preferable).[10] Such a policy would make internships significantly more accessible. If interns were paid the real living wage (an hourly rate linked to the actual cost of living),[11] then an intern would earn £1488 for a typical four-week internship, meaning they shouldn't need to dip into savings (which they might not have) or borrow money in order to complete an internship. Without such measures, completing an unpaid internship is simply not an option for many people who cannot afford to sustain themselves while working for nothing.

Completing an unpaid internship is essentially an investment. You invest your time – and the money needed for living costs – and in return you can make progress in your career. In other cases, making progress in one's career means risking financial hardship in the short term in order to reach one's aspirations in the long term. Unfortunately, such risks are not always spread evenly. A parallel can be drawn here with child labour. In England during the mid-19th century, around 60% of ten-year-old and a third of eight-year-old working-class boys were employed as child labourers.[12] They endured gruelling conditions and draconian discipline for pitifully low wages, but in spite of this, some argued that child labour was a good thing; after all, it enabled children to contribute to family incomes thereby lessening the effects of poverty.[13] According to this logic, measures that compelled children to go to school were deeply problematic. Surely forcing children to go to school rather than earn an honest living was profoundly immoral. These children had a right to earn rather than learn. Greater earnings meant more bread on the table. Who would dare deprive families of the opportunity for extra income?

The red flag warning us of the spurious nature of this argument is that families with the requisite means chose to forgo the benefits of additional income and instead prioritised their children's long-term prospects. But many families did not have a genuine choice between these two options. For many, forgoing the fruits of their children's labours could have plunged them into an unbearable state of poverty. The long-term gains were simply not worth the excruciating short-term pains threatened by extreme poverty.

Fortunately, education is now seen as a right and not a privilege (see Article 28 of The UN Convention on The Rights of The Child). And in wealthier countries at least, children are not coerced out of education and into the labour market in order to ameliorate family poverty. But while this injustice has been addressed to a significant extent, there are still cases where many people are unable to risk short-term financial pains in order to open up opportunities that confer long-term gains. Often, money is still necessary for unlocking opportunity.

Acting has been unmasked as a profession in which those from privileged backgrounds are highly over-represented[14] – around half of top actors are privately educated.[15] One key feature of this profession is the precariousness of work.[16] Generally, actors are contracted for a particular project (be that a play, film, TV production, etc.) rather than having long-term contracts.[17] This means there is always a risk of being out of work for considerable lengths of time: a big risk to take on, especially if you live in London – as many actors do – where rent or mortgage commitments are particularly demanding. Naturally, not all actors experience this precarity with equal intensity.[18] A report by Sam Friedman, Daniel Laurison and Dave O'Brien, for instance, found that: '…the ability of actors from privileged backgrounds to draw upon familial economic resources is pivotal in insulating them from much of the precarity and uncertainty associated with acting.'[19]

The fact that some people are able to draw upon such wealth while others are not means there are inherent inequalities in the level of financial risk people are forced to assume in order to reach their goals. To some extent, measures similar to statutorily mandated pay for interns may provide welcome support to actors and other creative professionals, particularly because the precariousness of these professions means that actors and creatives often take on unpaid work, a short-term pain that is more difficult for less privileged actors to endure.[20] But paying people properly when they are in work may not be enough on its own to address the consequences of the precariousness of the creative industries. As Friedman, Laurison and O'Brien have demonstrated, precarity itself generates the risk of financial hardship in the short term.[21] Many people from less affluent backgrounds may decide that it is not worth enduring this short-term pain in order to achieve the promises of any long-term gains. Just as child labourers were forced to forgo the rewards of an education and instead take a safer path (i.e., one that avoided hunger), many people who aspire to thrive in precarious professions are also pressured into taking less aspirational paths because the risks would otherwise be too great.[22]

But unlike the beneficiaries of child labour, I don't think it is acceptable for those who are not from privileged backgrounds to accept a lower reward in the long term in order to mitigate the risks of short-term pain. This is not a choice they should have to make. Measures ought to be put in place to ensure that everyone can manage during those difficult periods before the pay-off. And because the fundamental problem is that people may not have enough money to live on while following their dreams, the solution must include financial support. A simple but effective approach would be a career-progression loan system, which would allow aspiring professionals to borrow enough money to cover the cost of living comfortably (although not in luxury) while they worked hard towards achieving the lift-off point in their careers. The ideal system could be closely styled on student loans, which are designed so that debts are relatively manageable. For career-progression loans to be effective it is imperative that debts are similarly manageable. If aspiring professionals were anxious about incurring unmanageable debts, then the career-progression loans would not genuinely serve to ameliorate any short-term pain. Indeed, they could actually exacerbate the pain, particularly if there were credible fears that debts could spiral out of control.

Basing the career-progression loans on the student loans system is also justifiable. In both cases, loans should be manageable so that loanees can take up the opportunity to develop themselves – their skills, their experiences and their employability – without the fear of unmanageable debts. Just as students are, aspiring professionals should be given fair access to finance so that they can achieve their ambitions and, on a more pragmatic note, reach a point where they are in a position to pay back their loans.

Of course, career-progression loans could not be doled out without proper consideration for their financial viability. In practice, this may mean that loans would only be granted to applicants who can demonstrate that their careers are likely to reach lift-off in the near/medium future, and that they will hence be in a position to pay back their loans. This needn't be an issue from a social mobility standpoint. Better to establish a viable system than to have an unsustainable system that offered no means of equalising opportunity in the long run. The focus should therefore be on putting in place measures to support young people from all backgrounds to furnish their CVs with the kind of experiences/achievements that would indicate that they would be a safe bet to lend to. Lending institutions might want assurance, for instance, that an aspiring journalist had

had sufficient successes as an amateur writer to demonstrate that they actually had what it took to make it in journalism. That is perfectly sensible from their standpoint. From a social mobility standpoint, the priority then becomes to ensure that all aspiring journalists are supported to understand the kinds of resumes they need to build up in order to have a good chance of securing career-progression loans.

Where a lack of money itself prevents people from unlocking opportunities, money has to be part of the solution. As we have seen, this could mean actually paying people for their hard work, or it could mean making financial support available. But be warned, even these measures will not alleviate the most severe penalties experienced by those who are least well off.

Child poverty: the critical barrier

Let's not equivocate, equality of opportunity will not truly be achieved while child poverty plagues society. In the UK, 22% of people live in poverty – 4.6 million of whom are children.[23] For these young people, family income often does not even allow for good housing or healthy food.[24] The evidence is clear: life chances suffer as a result of child poverty.

In terms of measures of cognitive development, it has been shown that, on average, children who have grown up in persistent poverty during their early years score twenty percentile ranks lower than children who have never lived in poverty.[25] School absence rates are significantly higher for those young people enduring homelessness.[26] And a child living in poverty is almost three times more likely to experience mental health problems than children living in wealthier households.[27]

Destitute poverty inevitably takes its toll. Even if a young person goes to a brilliant school and is taught by inspirational teachers, if that child is hungry – note that 83% of teachers have reported witnessing signs of hunger among their students[28] – or burdened by poor mental health, they are not going to be able to seize the educational opportunities that are notionally available to them, certainly not to the same extent as peers who are not suffering in the same way. Even if a student's school has provided them with a state-of-the-art laptop on which to learn at home, their opportunities for effective learning will be diminished if they have no choice but to learn in an overcrowded and stressful environment.[29]

Some argue that the reason child poverty adversely affects people's life chances is that worklessness gives rise to less aspirational attitudes.[30] The solution hence lies in raising these children's aspirations, or so the argument goes. If this were true then the collective force of the solutions we have already discussed may succeed in counteracting the effects of child poverty on social mobility. But the attitudes and assumptions that are claimed to accompany growing up in a household without working adults are not the primary reasons why child poverty has such a toxic impact on one's life chances; indeed, over half of those living in poverty are in households in which at least one adult is in work.[31] The real issue is a lack of money.

An in-depth study from the London School of Economics, which involved a systematic review of evidence relating to child poverty in all EU and OECD countries, found that a lack of money affects children and families living in poverty in two key respects. Firstly, lacking money often means going without the basics – including nutritious food, which is 'critical for healthy brain development'.[32] The second factor is that constantly being in a state where you lack the means to acquire basic goods and resources leads to excessive levels of 'stress and anxiety'.[33] The report's authors, Kerris Cooper and Kitty Stewart, were clear in their conclusions: 'Money makes a difference to children's outcomes.'[34]

An excellent education and developmental opportunities from cradle to grave will, to an extent, be able to boost the life chances of young people who have grown up in abject poverty. But we cannot hope to truly level up opportunity unless the barriers people face are decisively levelled down. Those living in destitution will face far greater barriers in life than many of those who are privileged or even just comfortable. These barriers must be demolished if we are to achieve genuine social mobility. Governments should be working indefatigably to ensure that no child goes hungry or endures standards of housing that put their physical health at risk.[35] A child should never face such high levels of stress that their mental health suffers. And children shouldn't be left in situations where their families cannot make ends meet.

Child poverty is a critical barrier to social mobility, but not an insurmountable one. Child poverty can be reduced, and has been successfully reduced in the past. Between 1998 and 2005, 700,000 children in the UK were lifted out of poverty. A paper published in 2006 by the Institute for Fiscal Studies (IFS) pointed to both direct cash transfers to families with children, and measures that decreased the number of families without work, as factors contributing to this positive outcome. Both of these interventions served to raise incomes for the poorest families, thereby lifting a significant number of children out of poverty.[36]

I am sure that some people will consider that getting people into work rather than spending more on benefits would be the ideal way forward. A hand up is better than a hand out, etc. But remember, having working parents is by no means a watertight safeguard against the pains of child poverty. A plentiful supply of jobs that allow families to live comfortably above the poverty line may well be the ideal solution, and when this ambition is realised, then I would wholeheartedly agree that a hand up is better than a hand out. But that doesn't mean that benefits are not a valuable lever for achieving a dignified society in which all people can thrive and lead fulfilling lives. A system of direct cash transfers to in-need families is a viable way of addressing child poverty. And it is effective too, as shown by New Labour's successful implementation of such a system to lift nearly three quarters of a million children out of poverty. It should also be emphasised that the money needed for such a system should be better seen as an investment rather than an expenditure due to significant economic benefits associated with increasing social mobility. Child poverty mercilessly squanders potential. Money spent on recovering this potential will yield rewards in the long run.

Ending child poverty, by any means possible, is not an alternative or competing endeavour to the options we have discussed for upgrading social mobility. The eradication of child poverty is a prerequisite for allowing all people to determine the course of their own lives. I have no doubt that we will upgrade social mobility for the vast majority of people through purposeful uses of innovation, smashing glass ceilings and tearing down strongholds of unmerited elitism in the process. But if child poverty persists, as it inevitably will do without seismic shifts in how societies are organised, then measures to equalise opportunity will invariably overlook many people at the very bottom of society. This is not acceptable. Equality of opportunity means equality of opportunity. I repeat, equality of opportunity will not truly be achieved while child poverty plagues society.

CONCLUSION

I hope that this book has convinced you that social mobility is a goal towards which societies should strive, and that by harnessing advanced technologies we can make strides towards this goal.

Geared towards these ambitious objectives, this book was always intended as more of a call to arms than a passive exploration. In this spirit, I'll leave you with a final rallying cry.

For social mobility to be achieved, just one tantalisingly simple condition has to be met: a person's life chances must not be determined or unfairly influenced by their socioeconomic circumstances at birth. In other words, your background should be as irrelevant to your progress through life as the day of the week on which you were born.

Underneath all opposition to social mobility lies a pernicious indifference to whether or not this condition is met. No one can control the circumstances into which they are born, just as nobody can control their sex or their ethnicity. These attributes are part of who someone is, and as such should be recognised and celebrated, but they should not serve to limit or dictate the opportunities available to a person during their life.

In a just and fair world, if you were to walk into any boardroom, anywhere in the globe, what percentage of its inhabitants would you expect to be female? That's easy, 50%. If a person's gender had no bearing on their professional progress then, averaged across the population, men and women would have an equal chance of rising through the ranks to the boardroom. The ratio would hence tend towards 50:50.

Next question: what percentage of undergraduates at Russell Group universities – or students at drama schools, or high-flying apprentices, or teachers, nurses, graphic designers, management consultants, or any other role for that matter – would you expect to have been born into the bottom 20% (or quintile) of households based on income? In accordance with the reasoning above, the answer should be crystal clear: 20%. If a person's starting point did not determine or unfairly influence their progress in life (if it was as irrelevant as the day of the week on which they were born) then people born into this quintile would have the same chance on average of achieving any of these positions in society as people born into any other quintile. We'd therefore expect to see proportionate representation, which would mean 20% of people in any of these positions would have started life in the bottom quintile. Sadly, this isn't the case.

Society should not be configured in such a way as to penalise people based on factors that are beyond their control. People of all ethnicities and genders, and from any socioeconomic background, while also being valued for who they are and what makes them unique, should not have their life chances limited because of factors over which they have no influence.

As such, as we strive towards a more diverse, inclusive society, we cannot, in good conscience, ignore the stark inequalities of opportunity linked to socioeconomic circumstances. All people should have equal opportunities to flourish.

With regards to the role that technology has to play, I've not used these pages to make a 'snake oil'[1] sales pitch for the latest gadgetry. Instead, I have put forward numerous ways in which technologies, by virtue of their fundamental aptitudes, can address specific problems that give rise to social immobility.

In Chapter 2, I used the following table to summarise what technology has to offer.

Technology can...	Automate and augment human labour	Capture, analyse and draw insight from data	Connect people and expand their horizons
This is good for social mobility because...	Products/services that aid people's developments will become more affordable and more readily available Educational Institutions will become more productive and therefore more effective	Educators will be able to make better decisions, thereby enhancing their practice Institutions will be able to make fairer decisions at critical junctures	Access to productive networks and formative experiences will become more equal

Throughout this book I have shown how these principles can be put into practice. In Chapter 3, we saw that ITSs can drive down costs in the shadow education system, thereby opening up its benefits to all. In Chapter 4, we saw that technology's ability to automate tasks can be marshalled to allow teachers to use their time more effectively, and that its ability to extract insights from data can further enhance the efficacy of educational institutions.

In Chapter 5, we saw that technology can connect people to wider professional networks and experiences (via social media-style resources and VR/virtual programmes, respectively); that data-driven insights can be used to make recruitment fairer; and that data analytics can be used to help people navigate the labour market.

And in Chapters 6 and 7, we explored the potential benefits of a variety of other manifestations of these fundamental aptitudes of technology.

Because of these fundamental aptitudes, technology will be a powerful ally as we strive towards greater levels of social mobility. But remember, technologies are but humble tools. For a successful upgrade of social mobility, the effectiveness of the human-centred systems in which technologies are embedded is paramount. Strategies for achieving equality of excellence in our schools should centre upon unleashing the true potential of the teaching profession; the role of technology is to amplify the impacts of great teachers. Similarly, the most pressing problem with early years provision is not the current lack of innovative digital tools, it is the shortfall in highly qualified teachers; when/if more highly qualified teachers do enter the early-years sector they should be empowered with the best innovations on offer; the priority, however, is getting them into the sector in the first place. Careers education will advance immeasurably through the purposeful application of technology; but strong frameworks such as the Gatsby Benchmarks are still needed to give purpose to these innovations.

Innovative resources embedded within effective human-centred systems have the potential to genuinely move the dial, significantly increasing social mobility by restructuring the landscape of opportunity. But technology will not provide a silicon bullet solution.[2] Even if all the tech-driven solutions we have explored in these pages are implemented in full, work will still need to be done to achieve a sufficiently level playing field. While I firmly believe that innovative technologies can spearhead equality of excellence among schools with comparable resources, how far can we expect to bridge the educational divides between schools with vastly different resources at their disposal? Yes, technologies can make the labour market more equitable (and more productive) to a significant extent, but how can they defend against intentional nepotism? Illuminating the landscape of opportunity will have limited impact if certain individuals are still allowed to take shortcuts. And as I have already asserted, true equality of opportunity will remain chimerical unless the short-term pains needed to make long-term gains are ameliorated and, moreover, unless child poverty is vanquished once and for all.

Striving towards a fairer, more socially mobile society is no easy task. But we must take important strides in the right direction, and we have the tools to do so. Technology will not level the playing field entirely. But by purposefully utilising the innovations available to us, we can make real progress towards a society where a person's life chances are not unfairly influenced by the circumstances into which they were born.

Afterword

My exasperation with the UK's intolerably low levels of social mobility was the primary motivation for writing this book. Frustrated by the fact that public dialogue tended to either pessimistically fixate on the problems or act as though the problems could just be wished away, I resolved to identify and advocate for novel solutions so that progress could actually be made. By doing so I hoped to put forward at least a tentative roadmap that might help pave the way towards a fairer society.

I also intended to inject some optimism into the conversation around social mobility. I wanted people to realise that the problem of social immobility is not inevitable, and that the unfair distribution of life chances is not immutable. I still want that. But I must also acknowledge that the problems I set out to combat have since intensified due to the Covid-19 pandemic.

The crisis has set society back, and social immobility is now more entrenched than ever. After the adverse impacts of school closures, returning to pre-existing levels of educational inequality, while far from utopian, is now a key milestone. With that in mind, the innovations that we have discussed throughout this book should not wait in the wings until things have returned to normal; they should be at the forefront of the recovery.

In cases where schools are forced to close (either for all pupils, or for certain year groups), the students who miss out on time in the classroom should invariably have access to ITSs/adaptive learning platforms so that responsive, tailored learning continues to form part of their mixed educational diets. Moreover, these platforms should be available to every student, regardless of whether they are affected by further school closures, so that they can catch up on lost learning.

Now more than ever, teachers need to be maximising the amount of time they are spending on high-impact tasks. The burdens of low-impact tasks need to be removed as far as possible to enable them to do so.

And perhaps most importantly, the digital divide needs to be closed with urgency – not just addressed, closed – so that societal divisions are not exacerbated further during these difficult times.

Harnessing the full strength of advanced technology will be absolutely necessary if we are to face the challenges that lie ahead. But once we have overcome these challenges, this same strength will ensure that the new normal is a fairer and more empowering place in which to live.

REFERENCES

Introduction

1– Social Mobility Commission, 2017, *Time For Change: An Assessment of Government Policies on Social Mobility 1997-2017.*

2 – Ibid.

3 – Ibid.

4– Education Policy Institute, 2018, *Education in England: Annual Report 2018.*

5 – Social Mobility Commission, 2020, *Social Mobility Barometer Public attitudes to social mobility in the UK.*

6 – Milburn, Alan, 'The government is unable to commit to the social mobility challenge', *The Guardian*, December 2017, viewed at: www.theguardian.com/commentisfree/2017/dec/02/alan-milburn-government-not-comitted-to-social-mobility.

7 – The World Economic Forum, 2020, *The Global Social Mobility Report 2020 Equality, Opportunity and a New Economic Imperative.*

8 – Sutton Trust, Mobility Manifesto, 2019. Here, Sir Peter Lampl attributes this volatility, in part, to educational inequality.

9 – Weale, Sally, 'Ofsted chief links divide in education to "malaise" behind Brexit vote, *The Guardian*, December 2016, viewed at: www. theguardian.com/education/2016/dec/01/ofsted-chief-michael-wilshaw-links-divide-in-education-to-malaise-behind-brexit-vote; a similar point

is also made in Machin, S., Major, L. E., 2018, *Social Mobility and Its Enemies*, Pelican Books, which informed my thinking.

10 – Montacute, R., 2020, 'Social Mobility and Covid-19: Implications of the Covid-19 crisis for educational inequality', The Sutton Trust.

11 – Machin, S., Major, L. E., 2018, *Social Mobility and Its Enemies*, Pelican Books. And, The World Economic Forum, 2020, *The Global Social Mobility Report 2020 Equality, Opportunity and a New Economic Imperative.* My explanations of relative and absolute social mobility are informed by the explanations in these sources.

12 – Machin, S., Major, L. E., 2018, *Social Mobility and Its Enemies*, Pelican Books. Also, *Report from the Independent Commission on Social Mobility*, 2009, explains the distinction between absolute and relative social mobility in terms of the expansion of middle class jobs experienced after the second world war, highlighting that absolute social mobility can occur without relative social mobility necessarily occurring. This source also explains the link between social mobility and equality of opportunity.

13 – I'm alluding to the phrase "rise with your class not from it", which is attributed to John McLean. In Byrne. D, *Social mobility in the UK: what does the evidence tell us?*, Byrne uses this phrase to explain the concept of social mobility and to justify its importance. My aim is to invert the use of this phrase by highlighting that inequalities of opportunity can persist despite generational improvements in prosperity.

14 – oecdedutoday.com/coronavirus-future-learning-artificial-intelligence-ai/.

15 – Cullinane, C., Montacute, R., 2020, 'COVID-19 and Social Mobility Impact Brief #1: School Shutdown', The Sutton Trust.

16 – Ibid.

17 – Johnson, P., 2020, 'School closures have put an entire generation at a huge disadvantage', Institute for Fiscal Studies, May 2020, viewed at www.ifs.org.uk/publications/14858.

18 – Throughout the book, I emphasise the principle that people's life chances should not be unfairly influenced by their circumstances at birth. The idea behind and wording of this principle is informed by Teach

First (who state that 'no child's educational success should be limited by their socioeconomic background') and Klaus Schwab (who has stated that 'an individual's chances in life remain disproportionately influenced by their starting point—their socio-economic status at birth'). Given that my argument in favour of social mobility centres around the idea that individuals should have full control over their own lives, and that circumstances outside of their control should have minimal influence, I have chosen to formulate this principle in terms of circumstances not having 'unfair influences' on people's life chances. I interpret 'limit' to imply that circumstances could steer the trajectory of people's lives as long as this was not in a negative way; and I interpret 'disproportionate' to imply that life chances might be influenced by circumstances, but not as much as by other factors. However, I interpret 'unfairly influence' as a broad formulation, which reflects my belief that circumstances should have almost no impact on a person's life chances.

Chapter I

1 – Machin, S., Major, L. E., 2018, *Social Mobility and Its Enemies*, Pelican Books. And The World Economic Forum, 2020, *The Global Social Mobility Report 2020 Equality, Opportunity and a New Economic Imperative*. My explanations of the concept of and interpretations of IGE are informed by these sources.

2 – Corak, M., 2016, 'Inequality from Generation to Generation: The United States in Comparison', IZA Institute of Labor Economics. Note that further studies have provided a different value for the UK's IGE.

3 – Machin, S., Major, L. E., 2018, *Social Mobility and Its Enemies*, Pelican Books. Here the authors explain how the UK's IGE can be interpreted.

4 – The World Economic Forum, 2020, *The Global Social Mobility Report 2020 Equality, Opportunity and a New Economic Imperative*. Here it is argued that in many economies presently, one's background 'predetermines' their level of education, their options and their earnings.

Here I am specifically talking about hypothetical societies with an IGE of 1, and I use the word predetermine in the most literal sense.

5 – Social Mobility Commission, 2019, *State of the Nation 2018-2019.*

6 – Ibid.

7 – Teach First, 2016, *The Progression Report.*

8 – Social Mobility Commission, 2019, *State of the Nation 2018-2019.*

9 – Social Mobility Commission and The Sutton Trust, 2019, *Elitist Britain.*

10 – Kershaw, Alison, 'Private school fees reach £17,000 per year on average', *The Independent,* April 2018, viewed at www.independent.co.uk/news/education/education-news/private-school-fees-rise-average-year-inflation-isc-census-parents-term-costs-a8325001.html.

11 – Social Mobility Commission and The Sutton Trust, 2019, *Elitist Britain.*

12 – Sellgren, K., Salary premium' for private school pupils', *BBC News,* July 2014, viewed at www.bbc.co.uk/news/education-28125416.

13 – Coe, R., Little, J., Ndaji, F., 2016, *A comparison of Academic Achievement in Independent and State Schools*, report for the Independent Schools Council, published by Centre for Evaluation and Monitoring and Durham University. As discussed in Cassidy. S, 'Private school pupils "receive equivalent of two years" extra education', *The Independent*, February 2016.

14 – Cullinane, C., Montacute, R., 2018, 'Access to Advantage: The influence of schools and place on admissions to top universities', The Sutton Trust.

15 – research-repository.st-andrews.ac.uk/bitstream/handle/10023/9088/Sachs_2016_TRE_FairEquality_AAM.pdf?sequence=1 (viewed on 30 October 2020).

16 – Cribb, J., 2013, *Income Inequality in the UK*, Institute for Fiscal Studies (IFS), viewed at www.ifs.org.uk/docs/ER_JC_2013.pdf.

17 – Perfect, D., 2011, *Gender Pay Gaps*, Equality and Human Rights Commission Briefing, paper 2.

18 – Teach First, 2017, *Impossible? Social Mobility and the Seemingly Unbreakable Class Ceiling.*

19 – CIPD, 2020, Gender Pay Gap Reporting, viewed at www.cipd.co.uk/ Images/gender-pay-gap-reporting-2020_tcm18-19647.pdf.

20 – Wilkinson, R. D., Pickett, K., 2009, *The spirit level: Why more equal societies almost always do better,* Allen Lane/Penguin Group UK; Bloomsbury Publishing.

21 – The Great Gatsby Curve was introduced in 2012 by then chairman of the Council of Economic Advisers, Alan Krueger (obamawhitehouse. archives.gov/blog/2013/06/11/what-great-gatsby-curve#:~:text=The%20 Great%20Gatsby%20Curve%20illustrates,ladder%20compared%20 to%20their%20parents). The Great Gatsby Curve, and its history, is discussed in detail in *Social Mobility and its Enemies* (Machin, S., Major, L.E.). Here I aim to just provide an overview. Note that my discussions of how France compares to Canada draw upon insights from *Social Mobility and its Enemies* into how the UK compares to Canada/Australia. The Great Gatsby Curve is also discussed in The World Economic Forum, 2020, *The Global Social Mobility Report 2020 Equality, Opportunity and a New Economic Imperative.* My understanding and my explanation of the curve is informed by both of these sources.

22 – Graph was created by Tom Moule, using data for Gini coefficients from the World Bank (viewed at databank.worldbank.org/reports. aspx?source=2&series=SI.POV.GINI&country=) and using data for IGE from Corak (viewed at ftp.iza.org/dp9929.pdf). Corak's data on IGE is from 2006. The data used for Gini Index generally comes from the next available year (in most cases 2011) from the World Bank's database. My version of the graph is not intended to be an accurate or up-to-date representation of the exact relationship between inequality and social mobility. It is intended to show that there is a reasonably strong correlation between these factors.

23 – The World Economic Forum, 2020, *The Global Social Mobility Report 2020: Equality, Opportunity and a New Economic Imperative.*

24 – Machin, S., Major, L. E., 2018, *Social Mobility and Its Enemies*, Pelican Books.

25 – Ibid. The authors explain that all people would have a 20% chance of being in each of the quintiles. This fact can be worked out a priori

via the definition of equality of opportunity, which would necessitate proportionate representation if fulfilled.

26 – Ibid.

Chapter 2

1 – Seldon, A., 2018, *The Fourth Education Revolution: Will Artificial Intelligence liberate or infantilise humanity*, The University of Buckingham Press.

2 – The Boston Consulting Group and The Sutton Trust, 2017, *The State of Social Mobility in the UK*. Also, The World Economic Forum, 2020, *The Global Social Mobility Report 2020 Equality, Opportunity and a New Economic Imperative,* explains that professional networks and social capital are contributing factors to social mobility.

3 – Anissa, N., Baker, T., Smith, L., 2019, 'Educ-AI-tion Rebooted: Exploring the future of artificial intelligence in schools and colleges,' *NESTA*.

4 – See chapter 4.

5 – See chapters 5 and 6.

6 – Granovetter, M., 1974, *Getting a Job: A study of Contacts and Careers,* Cambridge, MA: Harvard Univ. Press, as referred to in Lin. N, *Social Networks and Status Attainment,* 1999.

7 – Pew Research Center, 2006, *The Strength of Internet Ties*, viewed at www.pewresearch.org/internet/2006/01/25/the-strength-of-internet-ties/.

8 – See Chapter 5 for examples.

9 – esrc.ukri.org/about-us/50-years-of-esrc/50-achievements/the-weak-ties-of-social-networks/, which discusses Granovetter, M., 'The Strength of Weak Ties', *American Journal of Sociology*, Vol. 78, No. 6 (May, 1973), pp. 1360-1380. The former source also refers to Granovetter's finding that that job opportunities were more likely to be sourced through weak ties than strong ties.

10 – esrc.ukri.org/about-us/50-years-of-esrc/50-achievements/the-weak-ties-of-social-networks/ and Lin. N, *Social Networks and Status*

Attainment, 1999. Here Granovetter is credited for developing a network theory for the flow of information.

11 – blogs.ubc.ca/etec540sept10/2010/10/30/printing-press-and-its-impact-on-literacy/ and Seldon, A., 2018, *The Fourth Education Revolution: Will Artificial Intelligence liberate or infantilise humanity*, The University of Buckingham Press. In the former source, the author explains that, before the printing press, the fact that books were handwritten led to them being expensive, which resulted in a situation in which book ownership, and therefore literacy, was dominated by the rich. In the latter source, Seldon describes how the printing press transformed the production of books, discusses how Gutenberg is considered to have invented the press, and notes the printing press's role in the Reformation. My introduction of the printing press as an example is influenced by Seldon's thinking around its revolutionary impact.

12 – blogs.ubc.ca/etec540sept10/2010/10/30/printing-press-and-its-impact-on-literacy/ (viewed on 30 October 2020). That the printing press played a role in facilitating the Reformation, Renaissance, and the Scientific Revolution is credited to Elizabeth Eisenstein.

13 – Seldon, A., 2018, *The Fourth Education Revolution: Will Artificial Intelligence liberate or infantilise humanity*, The University of Buckingham Press.

14 – blogs.ubc.ca/etec540sept10/2010/10/30printing-press-and-its-impact-on-literacy/.

15 – Government Digital Service and Office for Artificial Intelligence,2019. *A Guide to Using Artificial Intelligence in the Public Sector,* viewed at www.gov. uk/government/publications/understanding-artificial-intelligence/a-guide-to-using-artificial-intelligence-in-the-public-sector#:~:text=Defining%20 artificial%20intelligence,-At%20its%20core&text=AI%20can%20be%20 defined%20as,in%20large%20amounts%20of%20data.

16 – Lakhani, P., and Luckin, R., 2018, *The 'no nonsense' guide to artificial intelligence*, as seen at www.century.tech/news/no-nonsense-guide-to-ai/.

17 – Hogan, M., Whitmore, G., 'The top 20 artificial intelligence films – in pictures', *The Guardian*, January 2015: www.theguardian.com/culture/

gallery/2015/jan/08/the-top-20-artificial-intelligence-films-in-pictures. Note the examples of *2001: A Space Odyssey* and *The Terminator* are also given in *Intelligence Unleashed: An argument for AI in Education* (Luckin, Holmes, Griffiths and Forcier, 2016). Licence details available at creativecommons. org/licenses/by/4.0/. Report available at www.pearson.com/content/dam/ one-dot-com/one-dot-com/global/Files/about-pearson/innovation/open-ideas/ Intelligence-Unleashed-v15-Web.pdf.)

18 – Lakhani, P., and Luckin, R., 2018, *The 'no nonsense' guide to artificial intelligence*, as seen at www.century.tech/news/no-nonsense-guide-to-ai/.

19 – Ibid. Lakhani and Luckin use the phrase 'just around the corner' to describe media-driven perceptions of a robot invasion. Here, I use the phrase to genuinely speculate that general AI may be possible in the near future.

20 – Anderson. R. M, Twenty years on from Deep Blue vs Kasparov: how a chess match started the big data revolution, 2017, The Conversation, viewed at theconversation.com/twenty-years-on-from-deep-blue-vs-kasparov-how-a-chess-match-started-the-big-data-revolution-76882.

21 – www.darpa.mil/about-us/timeline/-grand-challenge-for-autonomous-vehicles (viewed on 30th October 2020). The Grand Challenge is also discussed in Luckin, R., Holmes, W., Griffiths, M., Forcier, L. B., 2016, *Intelligence Unleashed: An argument for AI in Education*, London: Pearson. Licence details available at creativecommons.org/licenses/by/4.0/. Report available at www.pearson.com/content/dam/one-dot-com/one-dot-com/ global/Files/about-pearson/innovation/open-ideas/Intelligence-Unleashed-v15-Web.pdf.

22 – Gabbatt, A., 'IBM computer Watson wins Jeopardy clash', *The Guardian,* February 2011, www.theguardian.com/technology/2011/ feb/17/ibm-computer-watson-wins-jeopardy. This article also suggests that Watson, unlike Deep Blue, demonstrates lateral thinking skills, as it is required to work with ambiguity.

23 – Lakhani, P., and Luckin, R., 2018, *The 'no nonsense' guide to artificial intelligence*, as seen at www.century.tech/news/no-nonsense-guide-to-ai/.

24 – Ibid.

25 – There are numerous examples of supervised machine learning being explained in terms of recognising images of dogs. For instance, medium. com/@bestpracticeAI/how-dogs-can-best-explain-machine-learning-an-executive-introduction-bed1374795b3 and www.saagie.com/blog/ machine-learning-for-grandmas/.

26 – www.ibm.com/cloud/learn/unsupervised-learning.

27 – medium.com/@bestpracticeAI/how-dogs-can-best-explain-machine-learning-an-executive-introduction-bed1374795b3.

28 – www.datarobot.com/wiki/unsupervised-machine-learning/.

29 – towardsdatascience.comartificial-intelligence-ai-terms-simply-explained-745c4734dc6c.

30 – deepmind.com/research/case-studies/alphago-the-story-so-far (viewed on 16 November 2020).

31 – ai.googleblog.com/2016/01/alphago-mastering-ancient-game-of-go. html and deepmind.com/research/case-studies/alphago-the-story-so-far (viewed on 30 October 2020).

32 – McKinsey Global Institute, 2018, *Notes from the AI Frontier: Applying AI for Social Good*, Discussion Paper, viewed at www.mckinsey. com/~/media/mckinsey/featured%20insights/artificial%20intelligence/ applying%20artificial%20intelligence%20for%20social%20good/mgi-applying-ai-for-social-good-discussion-paper-dec-2018.pdf.

33 – Kwok, R., 'AI Empowers Conservation Biology', *nature,* March 2019, viewed at www.nature.com/articles/d41586-019-00746-1. Note that Kwok describes the process of manually counting collisions as impractical, rather than as cumbersome and an inefficient use of a highly skilled researcher's time.

34 – Solly, M., 2019, 'New AI Camera Helps Conservationists Spot Elephant Poachers', *Smithsonian Mag*, January 2019, viewed at www.smithsonianmag.com/smart-news/new-ai-camera-helps-conservationists-spot-elephant-poachers-180971180/.

35 – Ibid.

36 – Simonite, T., 2017, 'Machine Learning Opens Up New Ways to Help People with Disabilities', *MIT Technology Review*, March 2017, viewed at

www.technologyreview.com/2017/03/23/68727/
machine-learning-opens-up-new-ways-to-help-disabled-people/.

37 – Snow, J., 2019, 'How People with Disabilities Are Using AI to Improve Their Lives', *PBS*, January 2019, viewed at www.pbs.org/wgbh/nova/articlepeople-with-disabilities-use-ai-to-improve-their-lives/.

38 – BBC News, August 2019, 'Google sign language AI turns hand gestures into speech', *BBC*, viewed at www.bbc.co.uk/news/technology-49410945.

39 – McKinsey and Company, How artificial intelligence will impact K-12 teachers, 2020:
www.mckinsey.com/industries/social-sector/our-insights/how-artificial-intelligence-will-impact-k-12-teachers.

40 – This point draws upon arguments made by Priya Lakhani, as seen in the following source: Lakhani, P., 'Why AI will NOT be teachers' downfall', *TES*, June 2019, viewed at www.tes.com/news/why-ai-will-not-be-teachers-downfall.

41 – The Economist Leader Article: 'Regulating the Internet Giants: The World's Most Valuable Resource is No Longer Oil, But Data', *The Economist*, May 2017, viewed at
www.economist.com/leaders/2017/05/06/the-worlds-most-valuable-resource-is-no-longer-oil-but-data.

42 – www.bernardmarr.com/default.asp?contentID=767 (viewed on 30th October 2020).

43 – Auschitzky, E., Hammer, M, Rajagopaul, A., 'How big data can improve manufacturing', *McKinsey and Company*, July 2014, viewed at www.mckinsey.com/business-functions/operations/our-insights/how-big-data-can-improve-manufacturing.

44 – Eggers, W. D., Kelkar, M., Sen, R., 2018, 'Building the Smart City', *Deloitte Center for Government Insights*, viewed at
www2.deloitte.com/content/dam/Deloitte/us/Documents/public-sector/us-fed-building-the-smart-city.pdf.

45 – www.besanttechnologies.com/big-data-vs-data-science (viewed on 30 October 2020).

46 – Ibid.

47 – Casey, K., 2019, 'How big data and AI work together', *The Enterprisers Project*, October 2019, viewed at enterprisersproject.com/article/2019/10/how-big-data-and-ai-work-together

48 – Yasinski, E., 2020, 'Big Data and Collaboration Seek to Fight COVID-19', *The Scientist*, July 2020, viewed at www.the-scientist.com/news-opinion/big-data-and-collaboration-seek-to-fight-covid-19-67759.

49 – Partington, R., 'Recession in real time: how big data can track the Covid slump', *The Observer*, August 2020, viewed at www.theguardian.com/business/2020/aug/08/recession-in-real-time-big-data-covid-slump-economy-unconventional-indicators.

50 – Shah, R., 'Introducing Data Science for Social Impact', *The Rockefeller Foundation*, January 2019, viewed at www.rockefellerfoundation.org/blog/introducing-data-science-social-impact/ (viewed on 30 October 2020).

51 – Higher Education Commission, 2016, *From Bricks to Clicks: The Potential of Data and Analytics in Higher Education*.

52 – Mullan, J., Peasgood, A., Sclater, N., April 2016, 'Learning Analytics in Higher Education: A review of UK and International Practice', *JISC*.

53 – Ibid.

54 – Ibid.

55 – In focusing on these two factors, my thinking is informed and influenced by that of thought leaders Priya Lakhani and Professor Rose Luckin. Lakhani has argued that, from a teacher's perspective, AI's role is to equip them with information and automate the more administrative tasks (as seen in the following article by Lakhani: www.tes.com/news/why-ai-will-not-be-teachers-downfall). Luckin's work, referred to later, has been instrumental in focusing the value of AI in education on its ability to draw useful insights from data.

56 – www.weforum.org/agenda/2018/01/8-ways-ai-can-help-save-the-planet/ (viewed on 3 November 2020). This source also refers to smart agriculture's role in ensuring the efficient uses of resources.

57 – Ibid., refers to the challenges caused by climate change. cordis. europa.eu/article/id/413531-unleashing-the-full-potential-of-smart-agriculture specifically refers to the issues of increasing demand for food and scarcity of arable land. This resource also discusses smart agriculture's responsiveness to fluctuations in weather conditions.

58 – Anderson, M., Turner, E., Vogels, E. A., 'The Virtues and Downsides of Online Dating', *Pew Research Center*, February 2020.

59 – As discussed in: Ferdman, A. R., 'How Well Online Dating Works, According to Someone Who Has Been Studying it for Years', *The Washington Post*, March 2016, viewed at www.washingtonpost.com/news/wonk/wp/2016/03/23/the-truth-about-online-dating-according-to-someone-who-has-been-studying-it-for-years/, and in Shashkevich, A., 'Meeting online has become the most popular way U.S. couples connect, Stanford sociologist finds', *Stanford News*, August 2019, viewed at news.stanford.edu/2019/08/21/online-dating-popular-way-u-s-couples-meet. Both sources also note that online dating platforms increase dating opportunities across the board.

60 – Hergovich, P., Ortega, J., 2018, 'The Strength of Absent Ties: Social Integration via Online Dating', viewed at arxiv.org/pdf/1709.10478.pdf.

61 – As discussed in: Ferdman, A. R., 'How Well Online Dating Works, According to Someone Who Has Been Studying it for Years', *The Washington Post*, March 2016, viewed at www.washingtonpost.com/news/wonk/wp/2016/03/23/the-truth-about-online-dating-according-to-someone-who-has-been-studying-it-for-years/, and in Shashkevich, A., 'Meeting online has become the most popular way – U.S. couples connect, Stanford sociologist finds', *Stanford News*, August 2019, viewed at news. stanford.edu/2019/08/21/online-dating-popular-way-u-s-couples-meet/.

62 – Acknowledging that the use of the terms 'get in' and 'get on' was influenced by the use of these terms in Friedman, S., Laurison, D., 2019, *The Class Ceiling: Why It Pays to Be Privileged*, 1st ed., Bristol University Press.

63 – news.stanford.edu/2018/10/17/virtual-reality-can-help-make-people-empathetic/ – quotation is from Fernanda Herrera.

64 – Szymczak, C., 'Virtuous Reality: Is there a place for Vr and AR in the "good space?"', *Unicef*, October 2016, viewed at www.unicef. org/innovation/xr/virtuous-reality-vr-in-the-good-space (viewed on 3 November 2020).

65 – Shashkevich, A., 'Virtual Reality can help make people empathetic, *Stanford News*, October 2018, viewed at news.stanford.edu/2018/10/17/ virtual-reality-can-help-make-people-empathetic/ referenced in www.pwc. co.uk/issues/intelligent-digital/virtual-reality-vr-augmented-reality-ar/three-ways-vr-can-change-the-world.html (both viewed on 3 November 2020).

66 – www.pwc.co.uk/issues/intelligent-digital/virtual-reality-vr-augmented-reality-ar/three-ways-vr-can-change-the-world.html (viewed on 3 November 2020).

Chapter 3

1 – Kirby, P., 2016, *Shadow Schooling: Private tuition and social mobility in the UK*, The Sutton Trust. The benefits of private tuition that I list are drawn from the benefits explained in this report.

2 – Ibid.

3 – The Sutton Trust, 2019, 'Private Tuition Polling 2019', *Ipsos MORI Young People Omnibus Survey* 2019.

4 – Jerrim, J., 'How much does private tutoring matter for grammar school admission?', FFT Education Datalab, March 2018, viewed at ffteducationdatalab.org.uk/2018/03/how-much-does-private-tutoring-matter-for-grammar-school-admissions/ (viewed on 6 November 2020).

5 – Fagg, H., 'Does private tuition, exacerbate educational inequality?' *Respublica*, June 2015, viewed at www.respublica.org.uk/disraeli-room-post/2015/06/02/does-private-tuition-exacerbate-educational-inequality/ (viewed on 6 November 2020).

6 – The Sutton Trust, *Grammar Schools: The Evidence Base*, 2015, viewed at www.faireducation.org.uk/evidence-base (viewed on 6 November 2020).

7 – Weale, S., 'An education arms race: inside the ultra-competitive world of private tutoring', *The Guardian*, December 2018, viewed at www.theguardian.com/education/2018/dec/05/an-education-arms-race-inside-the-ultra-competitive-world-of-private-tutoring. The tutoring of students for Oxbridge admissions tests is also refered to in Kirby, P., 2016, *Shadow Schooling: Private tuition and social mobility in the UK*, The Sutton Trust.

8 – Anissa, N., Baker, T., Smith, L., 2019, 'Educ-AI-tion Rebooted: Exploring the future of artificial intelligence in schools and colleges,' *NESTA*. The authors make the point that AI offers an accessible alternative to private tuition, not necessarily stating that it is the best candidate.

9 – Luckin, R., Holmes, W., Griffiths, M., Forcier, L. B., 2016, *Intelligence Unleashed: An argument for AI in Education*, London: Pearson. Licence details available at creativecommons.org/licenses/by/4.0/. Report available at www.pearson.com/content/dam/one-dot-com/one-dot-com/global/Files/about-pearson/innovation/open-ideas/Intelligence-Unleashed-v15-Web.pdf.

10 – IBL News, 'Pearson's AI Enabled Calculus App Provides Real-Time Feedback and Suggests Pathways', *IBL News,* November 2019, viewed at iblnews.org/pearsons-ai-enabled-calculus-app-provides-real-time-feedback-and-suggests-pathways/.

11 – www.pearson.com/us/higher-education/products-services-teaching/learning-engagement-tools/aida.html (viewed on 6 November 2020).

12 – Kulik, J.A., Fletcher,J.D., 'Effectiveness of Intelligent Tutoring Systems: A Meta-Analytical Review', *Review of Educational Research,* March 2016.

13 – Luckin, R., Holmes, W., Griffiths, M., Forcier, L. B., (2016), *Intelligence Unleashed. An argument for AI in Education*, London: Pearson. In this report, the authors outline the concept of these three models, and alternative approaches which utilise machine learning. My subsequent explanations of how ITSs support delivery of effective content via tailored pedagogical approaches are based upon insights from this report. Licence details available at creativecommons.org/licenses/by/4.0/. Report available at www.pearson.com/content/dam/one-dot-com/one-dot-com/global/Files/

about-pearson/innovation/open-ideas/Intelligence-Unleashed-v15-Web. pdf.

14 – squirrelai.com/product/ials (viewed on 23 November 2020).

15 – Beard, A., 'Can computers ever replace the classroom?' *The Guardian*, March 2020, viewed at www.theguardian.com/technology/2020/mar/19/can-computers-ever-replace-the-classroom (viewed on 18 November 2020).

16 – Hao, K. 'China has started a grand experiment in AI education. It could reshape how the world learns', *MIT Technology Review*, August 2019, viewed at www.technologyreview.com/2019/08/02/131198/china-squirrel-has-started-a-grand-experiment-in-ai-education-it-could-reshape-how-the/.

17 – Luckin, R., Holmes, W., Griffiths, M., Forcier, L. B., 2016, *Intelligence Unleashed. An argument for AI in Education*. London: Pearson. Licence details available at creativecommons.org/licenses/by/4.0/. Report available at www.pearson.com/content/dam/one-dot-com/one-dot-com/global/Files/about-pearson/innovation/open-ideas/Intelligence-Unleashed-v15-Web. pdf.

18 – Donnelly,C., J., 2015, *Enhancing Personalization within ASSISTtments*: *A Thesis Submitted to the Faculty of the Worcester Polytechnic Institute in partial fulfillment of the requirements for the Degree of Master of Science in Computer Science*, April 2015.

19 – Luckin, R., Holmes, W., Griffiths, M., Forcier, L. B., 2016, *Intelligence Unleashed. An argument for AI in Education*, London: Pearson. Licence details available at creativecommons.org/licenses/by/4.0/. Report available at www.pearson.com/content/dam/one-dot-com/one-dot-com/global/Files/about-pearson/innovation/open-ideas/Intelligence-Unleashed-v15-Web.pdf.

20 – The issue of variation in tutor quality is discussed in Education Endowment Foundation, Tutor Trust Primary: Evaluation report and Executive summary, 2015 and Education Endowment Foundation, Tutor Trust Secondary: Evaluation report and Executive summary, 2015.

21 – assets.publishing.service.gov.uk/government/uploads/system/uploads/attachment_data/file/812539/

Schools_Pupils_and_their_Characteristics_2019_Main_Text.pdf (viewed on 6 November 2020).

22 – Kirby, P., 2016, *Shadow Schooling: Private tuition and social mobility in the UK*, The Sutton Trust.

23 – educationendowmentfoundation.org.uk/covid-19-resources/national-tutoring-programme/#:~:text=The%20National%20Tutoring%20 Programme%20is%20a%20government%2Dfunded%2C%20 sector%2D,school%20closures%20on%20pupils'%20 learning.&text=It's%20estimated%20that%20around%2080,have%20 access%20to%20quality%20tuition. (viewed on 6 November 2020).

24 – Education Endowment Foundation, *Best Evidence on impact of school closures on the attainment gap*, June 2020, viewed at educationendowmentfoundation.org.uk/covid-19-resources/best-evidence-on-impact-of-school-closures-on-the-attainment-gap/ (viewed on 6 November 2020).

25 – Batty, D., 'UK school closures prompt boom in private tuition', *The Guardian*, March 2020, viewed at www.theguardian.com/education/2020/mar/27school-closures-prompt-boom-in-private-tuition-online-isolation.

26 – The phrase 'educational arms race' is used as part of the title of Chapter 4 of Machin and Major, *Social Mobility and Its Enemies*, Pelican Books; and has also been used by Sir Peter Lampl (as seen in www.theguardian.com/education/2018/dec/05/an-education-arms-race-inside-the-ultra-competitive-world-of-private-tutoring and Kirby, P., 2016, *Shadow Schooling: Private tuition and social mobility in the UK*, The Sutton Trust).

27 – Donnelly, M., Kumar, K., Lažetić, P., Sandoval-Hernandez, A. Whewal, S., 2019, *An Unequal Playing Field: Extra-Curricular Activities, Soft Skills and Social Mobility,* The Social Mobility Commission, Department of Education and Institute for Policy Research, University of Bath.

Chapter 4

1 – The phrase 'engine of social mobility' is used in Machin, S., Major, L. E., 2018, *Social Mobility and Its Enemies*, Pelican Books.

2 – Akhal, A., Bonetti, S., Crenna-Jennings, W., Hutchinson, J., 2019, 'Education in England: Annual Report 2019', The Education Policy Institute.

3 – Crenna-Jennings. W, 2018, *Key Drivers of The Disadvantage Gap Literature Review*, Education Policy Institute; also seen in evidence from the Sutton Trust published at publications.parliament.uk/pa/cm201719/cmselect/cmeduc/1006/100605.html.

4 – Economic and Social Research Council, *Education Vital for Social Mobility*, 2012, esrc.ukri.org/files/news-events-and-publications/evidence-briefings/education-vital-for-social-mobility/.

5 – Andrade, J., Cullinane,C., Hillary, J., McNamara, S., 'Selective Comprehensives: Admissions to high-attaining non-selective schools for disadvantaged pupils', *The Sutton Trust and NFER*, March 2017.

6 – Cullinane, C., Hillary, J., Van den Brande, J., 2019, '*Selective Comprehensives: Great Britain:* Access to top performing schools for disadvantaged pupils in Scotland, Wales and England', The Sutton Trust.

7 – Osborne, S., 'Poorest students in England nine times more likely to be in inadequate secondary schools, research shows', *The Independent*, August 2018, viewed at www.independent.co.uk/news/education/education-news/poor-children-schools-uk-poverty-secondary-education-state-angela-rayner-nick-gibb-a8500226.html.

8 – Andrade. J, Cullinane.C, Hillary. J, McNamara. S, *Selective Comprehensives: Admissions to high-attaining non-selective schools for disadvantaged pupils*, Sutton Trust and NFER, 2017. This source also discussed the fact that the increase in house prices in the catchments of top comprehensives leads to them becoming more socially exclusive. Further evidence can be seen Knight, R., 'PwC reveals that living near a bad school could knock up to £14,000 off your house price,', *Ideal Home*, October 2019, viewed at www.idealhome.co.uk/news/average-house-prices-near-a-good-school-236265.

9 – Machin, S., Major, L. E., 2018, *Social Mobility and Its Enemies*, Pelican Books.

10 – The All-Party Parliamentary Group on Social Mobility and The Sutton Trust, *Closing the Regional Attainment Gap*, 2018. Such disparities in the qualifications/levels of experience of teachers are also discussed in Weale, S., 'Schools with more poor students less likely to have qualified staff', *The Guardian*, June 2018, viewed at www.theguardian.com/education/2018/jun/11/schools-more-poor-students-less-likely-qualified-teaching-staff, and Allen. B, McInerney. L, 2019, *The Recruitment Gap: Attracting teachers to schools serving disadvantaged communities*, Sutton Trust; and in Allen. R, Mian. E, Sims. S, 2016, *Social inequalities in access to teachers*, Social Market Foundation Commission on Inequality in Education: Briefing 2.

11 – The All-Party Parliamentary Group on Social Mobility and The Sutton Trust, *Closing the Regional Attainment Gap*, 2018. The varying severity of the recruitment and retention crisis is also discussed in Allen, B., McInerney, L., 2019, 'The Recruitment Gap: Attracting teachers to schools serving disadvantaged communities', The Sutton Trust.

12 – The All-Party Parliamentary Group on Social Mobility and The Sutton Trust, *Closing the Regional Attainment Gap*, 2018. This figure is also cited in Allen, R., Mian, E., Sims, S., 2016, 'Social inequalities in access to teachers', *Social Market Foundation Commission on Inequality in Education: Briefing 2,* April 2016.

13 – Montacute. R., Cullinane., C., 2018, 'Parent Power 2018: How parents use financial and cultural resources to boost their children's chances of success', The Sutton Trust.

14 – Andrade. J, Cullinane.C, Hillary. J, McNamara. S, Selective Comprehensives: Admissions to high-attaining non-selective schools for disadvantaged pupils, Sutton Trust and NFER, 2017.

15 – Opper, I.M., 2019,'Teachers matter: Understanding Teachers' Impact on on Student Achievement,' *The Rand Corporation* viewed at www.rand.org/education-and-labor/projects/measuring-teacher-effectiveness/teachers-matter.html (viewed on 6 November 2020).

16 – Hattie, J., 2003, 'Teachers Make a Difference, What is the Research Evidence?' *Australian Council for Educational Research (ACER)*. Priya Lakhani has also highlighted Hattie's research as a key rationale for utilising technologies that can provide insights into learners' needs (as seen in www.leadermagazine.co.uk/articles/smarter_learning/). While Lakhani's focus is on Hattie's research around the importance of teachers understanding student performance, my focus is on Hattie's research around the importance of teacher's understanding the impacts of their own actions and decisions, so that they can adapt their practice accordingly.

17 – OECD, *Teachers Matter: Overview*, 2005, viewed at www.oecd.org/education/school/34990905.pdf.

18 – In focusing on these two factors, my thinking is informed and influenced by that of thought leaders Priya Lakhani and Professor Rose Luckin. Lakhani has argued that, from a teacher's perspective, AI's role is to equip them with information and automate the more administrative tasks (as seen in the following article by Lakhani: www.tes.com/news/why-ai-will-not-be-teachers-downfall). Luckin's work, referred to later, has been instrumental in highlighting that a key benefit of AI in education is its ability to draw useful insights from data. Furthermore, in The Institute for Ethical AI in Education'sInterim Report (www.buckingham.ac.uk/wp-content/uploads/2021/03/Interim-Report-The-Institute-for-Ethical-AI-in-Educations-Interim-Report-Towards-a-Shared-Vision-of-Ethical-AI-in-Education-1.pdf), the abilities of AI to both increase the capacity of educational organisations and to gain insight into learners' needs from data are given as two of the fundamental benefits of AI in education. Here I intend to develop upon the ideas put forward in The Interim Report and to apply them to the context of addressing social immobility. Specifically, I develop upon the ideas that technology can help to address the recruitment and retention crisis; that, as shown by the work of Black and Wiliam, Hattie, and The Education Endowment Foundation, information is a powerful resource for teaching and learning; and that technology may enable increased one-to-one time with teachers as well

as enabling personalised learning delivered directly through innovative software. I also develop upon the idea that these two capacities (automation and extracting insights) are combined and work in unison in advanced adaptive learning platforms.

19 – McKinsey and Company, How artificial intelligence will impact K-12 teachers, 2020: www.mckinsey.com/industries/social-sector/our-insights/how-artificial-intelligence-will-impact-k-12-teachers.

20 – Worth, J., 2018, 'Latest teacher retention statistics paint a bleak picture for teacher supply in England', *NFER*, June 2018, viewed at:,www. nfer.ac.uk/news-events/nfer-blogs/latest-teacher-retention-statistics-paint-a-bleak-picture-for-teacher-supply-in-england/.

21 – Weale, S., 'Fifth of teachers plan to leave profession within two years', *The Guardian*, April 2019, viewed at www. theguardian.com/education/2019/apr/16fifth-of-teachers-plan-to-leave-profession-within-two-years.

22 – Carr, J., 2019, 'Government misses secondary teacher training target for SEVENTH year in row', *Schools Week*, November 2019, viewed at schoolsweek.co.uk/government-misses-secondary-teacher-training-target-for-seventh-year-in-row/.

23 – 'Number of secondary pupils in England to rise 15% by 2027', *BBC News*, July 2018, viewed at www.bbc.co.uk/news/education-44809258.

24 – Adams, R., 'Pay more so teachers stay at disadvantaged schools, says thinktank', *The Guardian*, April 2016, viewed at www.theguardian.com/education/2016/apr/28/teachers-deprived-schools-pay-more-reduce-turnover-nick-clegg.

25 – 'Gordon Brown offers teachers £10,000 "golden handcuffs" under social mobility plans', *The Telegraph*, January 2009, viewed at www. telegraph.co.uk/news/politics/4226346/Gordon-Brown-offers-teachers-10000-golden-handcuffs-under-social-mobility-plans.html

26 – www.teachfirst.org.uk/our-impact (viewed on 16th November 2020).

27 – neu.org.uk/press-releases/state-education-workload.

28 – Department for Education, 2017, *Teacher Workload Survey 2016*, Research Report.

29 – Weale, S., '25% of teachers in England work more than 60 hours a week – study', *The Guardian*, September 2019, viewed at www.theguardian.com/education/2019/sep/18/25-of-teachers-in-england-work-more-than-60-hours-a-week-study.

30 – www.nfer.ac.uk/teacher-retention-and-turnover-research-research-update-4-how-do-teachers-compare-to-nurses-and-police-officers.

31 – Department for Education, 2017, *Teacher Workload Survey 2016*, Research Report.

32 – The Independent Teacher Workload Review Group, *Eliminating unnecessary workload around marking*, UK Government, 2016, viewed at www.gov.uk/government/publications/reducing-teacher-workload-marking-policy-review-group-report.

33 – Ibid. Findings on the adverse impact of workload from this report are also discussed in Seldon, A., 2018, *The Fourth Education Revolution: Will Artificial Intelligence liberate or infantilise humanity*, The University of Buckingham Press.

34 – Black, P., Wiliam, D., 2006, *Inside the Black Box: Raising Standards Through Classroom Assessment,* King's College London School of Education, viewed at score.hva.nl/Bronnen/Black,%20William,%20Inside%20the%20black%20box%20(2001).pdf.

35 – Hattie, J., 2003, 'Teachers Make a Difference, What is the Research Evidence?' Australian Council for Educational Research (ACER). Priya Lakhani has also highlighted Hattie's research as a key rationale for utilising technologies that can provide insights into learners' needs (as seen in www.leadermagazine.co.uk/articles/smarter_learning/). Whilst Lakhani's focus is on Hattie's research around the importance of teachers understanding student performance, my focus is on Hattie's research around the importance of teachers understanding the impacts of their own actions and decisions, so that they can adapt their practice accordingly.

36 – The phrases 'sage on the stage' and 'guide to the side' originate from Alison King.

37 – Black P. and D. Wiliam (1998), "Assessment and Classroom

Learning", Assessment in Education: Principles, Policy and Practice, CARFAX, Oxfordshire, Vol. 5, No. 1, pp. 7-74.

38 – Seldon, A., 2018, *The Fourth Education Revolution: Will Artificial Intelligence liberate or infantilise humanity*, The University of Buckingham Press.

39 – educationendowmentfoundation.org.uk/evidence-summaries/ teaching-learning-toolkit/individualised-instruction/.

40 – Black P. and D. Wiliam (1998), "Assessment and Classroom Learning", Assessment in Education: Principles, Policy and Practice, CARFAX, Oxfordshire, Vol. 5, No. 1, pp. 7-74.

41 – educationendowmentfoundation.org.uk/about/.

42 – educationendowmentfoundation.org.uk/evidence-summaries/ teaching-learning-toolkit/ (viewed on 6 November 2020).

43 – Webb, H., 2016, 'What does effective student feedback look like? Part 1', *SecEd*, September 2016, viewed at www.sec-ed.co.uk/best-practice/ what-does-effective-student-feedback-look-like-part-1/.

44 – Daw, P., Robinson, C., 2013, 'To the next level: improving secondary school teaching to outstanding', Research Report, CfBT Education Trust.

45 – Lakhani, P., Luckin, R, 2018, *The 'no nonsense' guide to artificial intelligence*, as seen at www.century.tech/news/no-nonsense-guide-to-ai/. Here, the authors explain how flipped learning brings the dual benefits of automated marking and increased insights into learning. The authors also reference the Education Endowment Foundation study led by Shireland Collegiate Academy that I discuss in this chapter.

46 – In Intelligence Unleashed (Luckin, R., Holmes, W., Griffiths, M., Forcier, L. B., 2016, *Intelligence Unleashed: An argument for AI in Education*, London: Pearson) the authors note that AI resources could be used to group students for collaborative tasks. Here, I am suggesting that teachers could do this themselves, given data insights from flipped learning tasks. Licence details available at creativecommons.org/licenses/by/4.0/. Report available at www.pearson.com/content/dam/one-dot-com/one-dot-com/global/Files/about-pearson/innovation/open-ideas/Intelligence-Unleashed-v15-Web.pdf.

47 – educationendowmentfoundation.org.uk/projects-and-evaluation/ projects/flipped-learning/ (viewed on 6 November 2020).

48 – 'Outsource marking' to cut teachers' workload', *BBC News*, April 2015, viewed at www.bbc.co.uk/news/education-32513932.

49 -Thacker, T., 'Century's role in the classroom', *Century*, 2018, viewed at; www.century.tech/news/century-in-the-classroom/ (viewed on 6 November 2020) .

50 – www.century.tech/news/century-tech-wins-prestigious-innovate-uk-grant-to-improve-education/ (viewed on 11 November 2020). The quote can also be seen at medium.com/@CENTURYTech/century-tech-wins-prestigious-innovate-uk-grant-to-improve-education-97c71db81c16 in an article written by CENTURY Tech.

51 – Anderson, J., 'A British start-up will put AI into 700 schools in Belgium', *Quartz*, March 2019, viewed at qz.com/1577451/century-tech-signs-deal-to-put-ai-in-700-classrooms-in-belgium/ (viewed on 18th November 2020). The statistic is also cited at my.optimus-education.com/sites/optimus-education. com/files/keynote_4_-_will_hall.pdf (viewed on 18 November 2020).

52 – www.gov.uk/government/news/damian-hinds-school-leaders-should-ditch-email-culture-to-cut-workload.

53 – aftabhussain.com/digital_assistants_for_everyone.html.

54 – Black, B., 'Exploring the potential use of AI in marking', *The Ofqual Blog*, January 2020, viewed at ofqual.blog.gov.uk/2020/01/09/exploring-the-potential-use-of-ai-in-marking/ (viewed on 6 November 2020).

55 – McKinsey and Company, 2020, *How artificial intelligence will impact K-12 teachers*, viewed at www.mckinsey.com/industries/social-sector/our-insights/how-artificial-intelligence-will-impact-k-12-teachers.

56 – Wyness, G., 2016, *Predicted grades: accuracy and impact*, University and College Union.

57 – Ibid.

58 – Mulholland, H., 2020, 'DfE to consult on post-qualification admissions as Williamson signals "radical change"', *Schools Week,* November 2020, viewed at schoolsweek.co.uk/dfe-to-consult-on-post-qualifications-admissions-as-williamson-signals-radical-change/.

59 – FE News, 2019 *ASCL response to Labour plans on university admissions*, viewed at www.fenews.co.uk/press-releases/33624-ascl-response-to-labour-plans-on-university-admissions.

60 – This is calculated based on statistics cited for the total number of hours worked by teachers on average from: Department for Education, 2017, *Teacher Workload Survey 2016*, Research Report.

61 – McKinsey and Company, 2020, *How artificial intelligence will impact K-12 teachers*, viewed at www.mckinsey.com/industries/social-sector/our-insights/how-artificial-intelligence-will-impact-k-12-teachers.

62 – Ibid.

63 – www.naht.org.uk/news-and-opinion/press-room/punitive-accountability-system-to-blame-for-teachers-leaving-profession-says-naht-responding-to-nfer-teacher-workforce-report/.

64 – Schools Week Reporter, 'Conservative manifesto 2019: the full list of schools policies', *Schools Week*, November 2019, viewed at schoolsweek.co.uk/conservative-manifesto-2019-the-full-list-of-schools-policies/.

65 – Luckin, R., Holmes, W., Griffiths, M., Forcier, L. B., 2016, *Intelligence Unleashed. An argument for AI in Education*. London: Pearson. Licence details available at creativecommons.org/licenses/by/4.0/. Report available at www.pearson.com/content/dam/one-dot-com/one-dot-com/global/Files/about-pearson/innovation/open-ideas/Intelligence-Unleashed-v15-Web.pdf. In the report, the authors explain multiple ways in which AI can be used to support collaborative learning.

66 – Ibid. This phrase alludes to a phrase used in *Intelligence Unleashed,* 'In one sense this is obvious – it is teachers who will be the orchestrators of when, and how, to use these AIED tools.' Here, I develop upon the phrase in order to demonstrate the concept of teachers' dual strategic and tactical roles. Licence details available at creativecommons.org/licenses/by/4.0/. Report available at www.pearson.com/content/dam/one-dot-com/one-dot-com/global/Files/about-pearson/innovation/open-ideas/Intelligence-Unleashed-v15-Web.pdf.

67 – Luckin, R., Holmes, W., Griffiths, M. Forcier, L. B., 2016, *Intelligence*

Unleashed. An argument for AI in Education. London: Pearson. Licence details available at creativecommons.org/licenses/by/4.0/. Report available at www.pearson.com/content/dam/one-dot-com/one-dot-com/global/Files/about-pearson/innovation/open-ideas/Intelligence-Unleashed-v15-Web.pdf.

68 – De Laat, M., Chamrada, M., Wegerif, R., 2008, 'Facilitate the facilitator: Awareness tools to support the moderator to facilitate online discussions for networked learning', *Proceedings of the 6th International Conference on Networked Learning* (pp. 80–86).

69 – Cukurova, M., Luckin, R., Millán, E., Mavrikis, M., 2018, 'The NISPI framework: Analysing collaborative problem-solving from students' physical interactions'. *Computers and Education*, January 2018, 116 pp. 93-109. 10.1016/j.compedu.2017.08.007.

70 – IBID. Here the authors argue that insights can be used to "shape and time" the support that teachers provide, and allow for teacher time to be prioritised.

71 – Priya Lakhani has described teachers as the most powerful person in the classroom. Here, I intend to highlight that teachers are themselves resources and are among the most powerful resources that students can benefit from.

72 – Cukurova, M., Luckin, R., Millán, E., Mavrikis, M., 2018, 'The NISPI framework: Analysing collaborative problem-solving from students' physical interactions'. *Computers and Education*, January 2018, 116 pp. 93-109. 10.1016/j.compedu.2017.08.007.

73 – Luckin, R, 2017, *Towards artificial intelligence-based assessment systems*, *Nature Human Behaviour*, January 2017. This principle is also described in Luckin et al., *Intelligence Unleashed. An argument for AI in Education..* Licence details available at creativecommons.org/licenses/by/4.0/. Report available at www.pearson.com/content/dam/one-dot-com/one-dot-com/global/Files/about-pearson/innovation/open-ideas/Intelligence-Unleashed-v15-Web.pdf.

74 – Ibid. Both sources describes how teachers and students benefit from open-learner models which provide deep, long-term insights into students'

needs. The use of the phrase 'under the magnifying glass' in this context is inspired by an observation that devices act as microscopes, enabling advanced insights into how people learn, as seen in *System Upgrade: realising the vision for UK education, Technology Enhanced Learning*. Note, I am more concerned with how teachers are empowered to support individual learners in the medium term, than by how technology can provide a long term understanding of the underlying ways in which all people learn.

75 – Professor Luckin explains this principle, as seen in epale.ec.europa. eu/en/blog/artificial-intelligence-cracks-open-black-box-learning.

76 – Dev,S., 'Innovative video tech improves learning outcomes', *Express Computer*, November 2019:
www.expresscomputer.in/industries/education/
innovative-video-tech-improves-learning-outcomes/43882/.

77 – This use of predictive analytics is explained in both Ekowo, M., Palmer. I., 2016, 'The Promise and Peril of Predictive Analytics in Higher Education', *New America*, October 2016, and also success.gsu.edu/
initiatives/gps-advising/#:~:text=A%20Strategic%20Approach,get%20
students%20back%20on%20track. The quotation is from the latter source.

78 – Ekowo,. M., Palmer, I., 2016, *The Promise and Peril of Predictive Analytics in Higher Education*, *New America,* October 2016.

79 – success.gsu.edu/initiatives/gps-advising/#:~:text=A%20Strategic%20
Approach,get%20students%20back%20on%20track.

80 – Ekowo and Palmer, M., Palmer, I., 2016, *The Promise and Peril of Predictive Analytics in Higher Education*, *New America,* October 2016.

81 – Acknowledging that the use of the word 'orchestration' is informed by a phrase used in *Intelligence Unleashed*, 'In one sense this is obvious – it is teachers who will be the orchestrators of when, and how, to use these AIEd tools.' Licence details available at creativecommons.org/licenses/by/4.0/. Report available at www.pearson.com/content/dam/one-dot-com/one-dot-com/global/Files/about-pearson/innovation/open-ideas/Intelligence-Unleashed-v15-Web.pdf.

82 – educationendowmentfoundation.org.uk/evidence-summaries/
teaching-learning-toolkit/individualised-instruction/ (viewed on November

6th 2020). The definition I provide of individualised learning is based on the EEF's definition.

83 – Acknowledging that the term 'one-size-fits-all', in the context of personalised learning, has been popularised by CENTURY tech, as seen in www.century.tech/news/no-nonsense-guide-to-ai/.

84 – educationendowmentfoundation.org.uk/evidence-summaries/teaching-learning-toolkit/individualised-instruction/ (viewed on 6 November 2020).

85 – Acknowledging that the phrase 'individualised learning on steroids' is not wholly original. Similar phrases have been used elsewhere, for instance: www.edutopia.org/blog/enhanced-learning-through-differentiated-technology-julie-stern uses the phrase 'differentiation on steroids' dpalank. wordpress.com/2017/07/17/individualized_learning_on_steroids/ uses the phrase 'individualised learning class (on steroids)'.

86 – Noting the similarity between my argument around full personalisation vs partial differentiation and that expressed in Lakhani, P., Luckin. R, *The 'no nonsense' guide to artificial intelligence*, as seen at www.century.tech/news/no-nonsense-guide-to-ai/. Note, here I am specifically arguing that technology in general allows teachers to build upon partial differentiation without technology; the argument in *The no nonsense guide to artificial intelligence* focuses on the differences between rules-based adaptive learning platforms and machine-learning-based platforms.

87 – www.century.tech/news/century-tech-wins-prestigious-innovate-uk-grant-to-improve-education/ This point also relates to insights from the EEF on the effects of immediacy of feedback on the efficacy of tech-based individualised learning: educationendowmentfoundation. org.uk/evidence-summariesteaching-learning-toolkit/individualised-instruction/.

88 – Ma, M., 2019, 'How does CENTURY's AI work?', *Century*, June 2019, views at: www.century.tech/news/how-does-centurys-ai-work/ viewed on 11 November 2020.

89 – www.century.tech/news/no-nonsense-guide-to-ai/.

90 – www.century.tech/testimonial/basingstoke-college-of-technology/ (viewed on 11 November 2020).

91 – www.century.tech/news/how-does-centurys-ai-work/ (viewed on 11 November 2020).

92 – www.century.tech/news/learning-at-century/ (viewed on 11 November 2020).

93 – Lakhani, P.,'Robots in the classroom? Separating truth from Science Fiction', Cobis, viewed at: www.cobis.org.uk/blog/robots-in-the-classroom-separating-truth-from-science-fiction (viewed on 11 November 2020).

94 – inspiringleadership.org/wp-content/uploads/2017/11/Alice-Little-Artificial-Intelligence-and-Data-In-Schools.pdf (viewed on 11 November 2020).

95 – www.capita-sims.co.uk/sites/default/files/2018-06/Century-Product-Guide-WEB.pdf (viewed on 11 November 2020). The point regarding immediate feedback is also made in www.century.tech/news/century-in-the-classroom/.

96 – www.century.tech/news/century-tech-wins-prestigious-innovate-uk-grant-to-improve-education/ (viewed on 18 November 2020).

97 – Beckingham. K, *The rise of personalised learning,* Education Technology, February 2020, viewed at edtechnology.co.uk/latest-news/rise-personalised-learning-education/. Here, Iona Clark, a curriculum specialist at CENTURY Tech, explains that technology can enable teachers to 'further personalise' their teaching.

98 – the ability of advanced platforms to support student reflection has been discussed in Luckin, R., 2017, *Towards artificial intelligence-based assessment systems, Nature Human Behaviour* and – Luckin, R., Holmes, W., Griffiths, M., Forcier, L. B., 2016, *Intelligence Unleashed: An argument for AI in Education.* Licence details available at creativecommons.org/licenses/by/4.0/. Report available at www.pearson.com/content/dam/one-dot-com/one-dot-com/global/Files/about-pearson/innovation/open-ideas/Intelligence-Unleashed-v15-Web.pdf.

99 – Luckin, R., 2017, *Towards artificial intelligence-based assessment systems, Nature Human Behaviour.* Acknowledging that the phrase 'open

the black box of learning', used and attributed earlier in this chapter, is from Luckin.

100 – Ibid.

101 – Luckin, R., Holmes, W., Griffiths, M., Forcier, L. B., 2016, *Intelligence Unleashed: An argument for AI in Education*. Licence details available at creativecommons.org/licenses/by/4.0/. Report available at www.pearson.com/content/dam/one-dot-com/one-dot-com/global/Files/about-pearson/innovation/open-ideas/Intelligence-Unleashed-v15-Web.pdf. In the report, the authors explain that AI will be able to 'leverage new insights in disciplines such as psychology and educational neuroscience to better understand the learning process, and so build more accurate models that are better able to predict – and influence – a learner's progress, motivation, and perseverance.' Here, I build upon this foundation with examples.

102 – mycognition.com/ (viewed on 11 November 2020).

103 – mycognition.com/how-it-works/ (viewed on 11 November 2020).

104 – Gilkey, R., Kilts, C., 2007, 'Cognitive Fitness', *Harvard Business Review*, November 2007, hbr.org/2007/11/cognitive-fitness.

105 – www.nhs.uk/apps-library/mycognition-home/.

106 – mycognition.com/case-studies/ See case study with Welsh Primary Schools (viewed on 11 November 2020).

107 – www.globalteacherprize.org/person?id=2673.

108 – Nesta, HegartyMaths, The Behavioural Insights Team, 2020, *Applying Behavioural Insights in EdTech: An incomplete guide*.

109 – www.instituteforgovernment.org.uk/explainers/nudge-unit (viewed on 11th November 2020).

110 – Nesta, HegartyMaths, The Behavioural Insights Team, 2020, *Applying Behavioural Insights in EdTech: An incomplete guide*.

111 – Johnson, W. L., Valente, A., 2009, 'Tactical Language and Culture Training Systems: Using AI to Teach Foreign Languages and Cultures'. *AI Magazine*, Summer 2009, *30*(2), 72. doi.org/10.1609/aimag.v30i2.2240.

112 – Ibid.

113 – Ibid.

114 – digitalworksgroup.com/speech-performance-analytics-startup-wins-best-innovation-natural-language-processing/ (viewed on 11 November 2020).

115 – www.gweekspeech.com/ (viewed on 11 November 2020).

116 – www.gweekspeech.com/education/ (viewed on 16 November 2020).

117 – epale.ec.europa.eu/en/blog/artificial-intelligence-cracks-open-black-box-learning Professor Luckin suggests that AI may make time available for offline tuition as well.

118 – educationendowmentfoundation.org.uk/evidence-summaries/teaching-learning-toolkit/one-to-one-tuition/ (viewed on 11th November 2020). The point is also made in The Interim Report of The Institute for Ethical AI in Education (www.buckingham.ac.uk/wp-content/uploads/2021/03/Interim-Report-The-Institute-for-Ethical-AI-in-Educations-Interim-Report-Towards-a-Shared-Vision-of-Ethical-AI-in-Education-1.pdf).

119 – www.mckinsey.com/industries/social-sector/our-insights/how-artificial-intelligence-will-impact-k-12-teachers (viewed on 11 November 2020).

120 – Seldon, A., 2018, *The Fourth Education Revolution: Will Artificial Intelligence liberate or infantilise humanity*, The University of Buckingham Press.

121 – Ibid.

Chapter 5

1 – Social Mobility Commission and The Sutton Trust, 2019, *Elitist Britain*, June 2019.

2 – Social Mobility Commission, 2019, *State of the Nation 2018-2019*, April 2019.

3 – The Sutton Trust, *Mobility Manifesto, 2010*

4 – Oxera, 2017, 'Social Mobility and Economic Successes', Prepared for

The Sutton Trust, June 2017; statistic also cited in www.oxera.com/agenda/
hidden-talent-the-economic-benefits-of-social-mobility/.

5 – Partington, R., 'Coronavirus bill has cost UK government £210bn, spending watchdog says', *The Guardian*, September 2020 viewed at www. theguardian.com/politics/2020/sep/08/uks-public-spending-watchdog-estimates-210bn-coronavirus-bill.

6 – www.oxera.com/agenda/hidden-talent-the-economic-benefits-of-social-mobility/ (viewed on 15 November 2020).

7 – Coughlan, S., 'Career ambitions "already limited by age of seven"', *BBC News*, October 2019, viewed at www.bbc.co.uk/news/amp/education-50042459.

8 – www.gatsby.org.uk/education/focus-areas/good-career-guidance. The report discusses the fact that some young people have internalised feelings about where people like them might fit in. The report puts the phrase 'people like them' in quotation marks, however, I do not feel this is appropriate as I believe that sometimes people are made to feel that people like them should set aspirations lower. Putting the phrase in quotations might imply that I don't fully endorse this sentiment.

9 – Ibid. My understanding of the timeline of the Gatsby Benchmarks' impacts was informed by the following source: complete-careers.com/gatsby-benchmarks/.

10 – The Department for Education, 2017, *Careers strategy: making the most of everyone's skills and talents*, December 2017, viewed at assets.publishing.service.gov.uk/government/uploads/system/uploads/attachment_data/file/664319/Careers_strategy.pdf.

11 – www.gov.uk/government/news/careers-guidance-in-schools-not-working-well-enough. Ofsted's concerns were directly mentioned in Good Careers Guidance.

12 – Holman, J., 2019, 'Careers leaders – the critical factor in good career guidance', *The Careers and Enterprise Company*, July 2019, viewed at: www.careersandenterprise.co.uk/news/careers-leaders-critical-factor-good-career-guidance.

13 – The Careers and Enterprise Company, 2019, *State of the Nation 2019*.

14 – Acknowledging that the phrase "you can't be what you can't see" is also used in www.bbc.co.uk/news/amp/education-50042459, by Andreas Schleicher.

15 – www.linklaters.com/en/about-us/news-and-deals/news/2019/june/ linklaters-launches-first-of-its-kind-online-legal-internship-open-to-all-uk-students (viewed on 18 November 2020).

16 – Ibid.

17 – Ibid.

18 – Ibid.

19 – The extension of the opportunity to complete the virtual internship with Linklaters was reported in: -www.legalcheek.com/2020/10/linklaters-extends-virtual-internship-to-sixth-formers/, www.lawgazette.co.uk/news/ teenagers-offered-virtual-work-experience-at-linklaters-/5106160.article and www.lawcareers.net/Explore/News/A-level-students-offered-virtual-work-experience-at-Linklaters-28102020. These three website sources were all viewed on 18 November 2020.

20 – Luckin, R., Holmes, W., Griffiths, M., & Forcier, L. B., 2016, *Intelligence Unleashed. An argument for AI in Education.* Licence details available at creativecommons.org/licenses/by/4.0/. Report available at www. pearson.com/content/dam/one-dot-com/one-dot-com/global/Files/about-pearson/innovation/open-ideas/Intelligence-Unleashed-v15-Web.pdf.

21 – visualise.com/case-study/british-army-vr-recruitment-experience (viewed on 15 November 2020).

22 – www.inavateonthenet.net/features/article/the-vr-headsets-saving-lives (viewed on 15 November 2020).

23 – services.airbus.com/en/newsroom/stories/2019/12/airbus-brings-cockpit-to-you-with-new-virtual-reality-flight-trainer.html.

24 – prospela.com/about/ (viewed on 6 November 2020).

25 – prospela.com/ (viewed on 6 November 2020).

26 – King, S.L., 2018, 'Revealed: The 2018 Teach First Innovation Award winners', *Schools Week,* March 2018.

27 The Careers and Enterprise Company, 2017, *The Gatsby Benchmark Toolkit for Schools :Practical information and guidance for schools*, viewed

at www.careersandenterprise.co.uk/sites/default/files/uploaded/1041_ gatsby_toolkit_for_schools_final.pdf. My point is deduced from their point that students with the least social capital have most to gain.

28 – Learning and Skills Council, 2004, 'LMI Matters! Understanding labour market information', *Department for Education and Skills.*

29 – Orlik, J., 2020, 'Workers are struggling to adapt to an uncertain world', *Nesta*, August 2020,www.nesta.org.uk/blog/workers-are-struggling-adapt-uncertain-world/ In this blogpost the term 'real-time map' is used and explained.

30 – Douglas, R., Orlik, J., Rhode, M., Scott, R., Ward, P., 2020, 'Finding Opportunities in Uncertainty: The information and support that workers need to navigate a changing job market', *Nesta*, July 2020.

31 – Ibid.

32 – Social Mobility and Child Poverty Commission, 2013, *Business and Social Mobility: a Manifesto for Change,* October 2013.

33 – www.accaglobal.com/uk/en/member/member/accounting-business/2018/03/insights/social-mobility.html viewed on November 6th 2020.

34 – Mokades, R., 'Recruitment: don't underestimate skills because of background', *Personnel Today*, April, 2018 viewed at www.personneltoday. com/hr/recruitment-underestimate-skills-background/ (viewed on 6 November 2020).

35 – www.noticed.org.uk/contextual-recruitment-system-important/ (viewed on 6 November 2020).

36 – www.personneltoday.com/hr/recruitment-underestimate-skills-background/ (viewed on 17 November 2020).

37 – contextualrecruitment.co.uk.

38 – Ibid.

39 – Ibid. Statistic also cited at www.rarerecruitment.co.uk,

40 – Friedman, S., Laurison, D., 2019, *The Class Ceiling: Why It Pays to Be Privileged*, 1st ed., Bristol University Press.

41 – Ibid. At different points in the book, the authors use the phrases/words that appear in quotation marks here in reference to feelings of not fitting in.

42 – Savage, M., 2015, *Social Class in the 21st Century*, London: Pelican. Note the term 'profound emotional imprint' is also used in *The Class Ceiling*.

43 – Friedman, S., ,2016, 'Habitus clivé and the emotional imprint of social mobility', *The Sociological Review*, 64 (1). pp. 129-147. ISSN 0038-0261. Note, the term 'considerable psychological price' is also used in *The Class Ceiling*.

44– Ibid. The fact that social mobility can lead to feelings of abandonment and tensions with family is discussed here.

45 – In *The Class Ceiling*, interviewees commented that they felt as if they did not belong in certain professional contexts; the authors discuss feelings of anxiety around this.

46 – Address at Rice University on the Nation's Space Effort, 1962.

47 – Friedman S., Laurison, D., 2019, *The Class Ceiling: Why It Pays to Be Privileged*, 1st ed., Bristol University Press.

48 – Ibid.

Chapter 6

1 – Andrews, J., Hutchinson, J., Robinson, D., 2017, 'Closing the Gap? Trends in Educational Attainment and Disadvantage', *Education Policy Institute*, August 2017. Also seen in Crenna-Jennings. W, 2018, *Key Drivers of The Disadvantage Gap Literature Review*, Education Policy Institute.

2 – Department for Education, 2017, *Unlocking Talent and Fulfilling Potential,* December 2017.

3 – Crenna-Jennings. W, 2018, *Key Drivers of The Disadvantage Gap Literature Review*, Education Policy Institute.

4 – Ibid.

5 – Noting that the term 'silicon bullet' has been used previously and has been attributed to Lynch, T. L., 2015, *The Hidden Role of Software in Educational Research: Policy to Practice*, , NY: Routledge. As viewed in Williamson, B., 2018, 'Silicon startup schools: technocracy, algorithmic

imaginaries and venture philanthropy in corporate education reform', *Critical Studies in Education*, 59:2, 218-236.

6 – Quotation is referenced in: Perlman Robinson, J., Petrova, D., 2015, 'Getting millions to learn: The impact of *Sesame Street* around the world', *Brookings*, March 2015 (viewed at www.brookings.edu/blog/education-plus-development/2015/03/18/getting-millions-to-learn-the-impact-of-sesame-street-around-the-world/) and is attributed to Mares, M. and Pan, Z, 2013, 'Effects of *Sesame Street*: A meta-analysis of children's learning in 15 countries.' *Journal of Applied Developmental Psychology* 34 (2013): 140-151.

7 – Quotation is referenced in: Timsit, A., 2019, 'This is how *Sesame Street* is improving children's education across the world', *World Economic Forum* and *Quartz*, February 2019 (viewed at www.weforum.org/agenda/2019/02/economists-explain-why-kids-who-watched-sesame-street-did-better-in-school) and is attributed to Kearney, M. S., and Levine, P.B., 2019, 'Early Childhood Education by Television: Lessons from *Sesame Street*.' *American Economic Journal: Applied Economics*, 11 (1): 318-50, January 2019.

8 – Timsit, A., 2019, 'This is how *Sesame Street* is improving children's education across the world', *World Economic Forum* and *Quartz,* February 2019 (viewed at www.weforum.org/agenda/2019/02/economists-explain-why-kids-who-watched-sesame-street-did-better-in-school).

9 – Ibid.

10 – Ibid.

11 – www.ibm.com/watson/education/sesame-street (viewed on 9 November 2020).

12 – www.boltoncollege.ac.uk/latest-news/praise-for-ada-bolton-colleges-chatbot/ (viewed on 9 November 2020).

13 – Gabbat, A., 'IBM computer Watson wins Jeopardy clash', *The Guardian*, February 2011, viewed at www.theguardian.com/technology/2011/feb/17/ibm-computer-watson-wins-jeopardy.

14 – www.sesameworkshop.org/what-we-do/schools/ibm-watson (viewed on 5 December 2020), and seen in www.ibm.com/blogs/think/2017/06/sesame-street/.

15 – www.ibm.com/blogs/think/2017/06/sesame-street/ (viewed on 9 November 2020).

16 – www.ibm.com/watson/education/sesame-street and www. sesameworkshop.org/what-we-do/schools/ibm-watson.

17 – www.oyalabs.com/ (viewed on 9 November 2020).

18 – www.oyalabs.com/science (viewed on 17 November 2020).

19 www.oyalabs.com/ (viewed on 9 November 2020).

20 – Waldfogel. J, and Washbrook. E, *Low income and early cognitive development in the UK*, The Sutton Trust, 2010. The Sutton Trust, 2015, *Mobility Manifesto*.

21 – www.suttontrust.com/wp-content/uploads/2019/12/EasyPeasy-Evaluation_FINAL.pdf.

22 – Jelley, F., Sylva, K., 2018; 'Easy Peasy,' *Easy Peasy, Esmée Fairbairn Foundation, Newham London, The Sutton Trust, The University of Oxford.* www.suttontrust.com/wp-content/uploads/2019/12/EasyPeasyNewham-FINAL.pdf.

23 – Ibid.

24 – Ibid., and also discussed in www.suttontrust.com/wp-content/ uploads/2019/12/EasyPeasy-Evaluation_FINAL.pdf. The former source specifically discusses the impacts on parents' sense of control.

25 – Jones, A., Moody, A., Parker, M., Skibbe, L., 2014, 'Use of Electronic Storybooks to Promote Print Awareness in Preschoolers who are Living in Poverty', *Journal of Literacy and Technology*, Volume 15, Number 3, ISSN: 1535-0975, December 2014.

26 – www.dyslexia.uk.net/assistive-technology/assistive-technology-reading-writing-spelling/audio-books-ebooks/ (viewed on 9 November 2020).

27 – The Sutton Trust, Mobility Manifesto, 2019. Here it is argued that there has been an 'ongoing shift' in policy from quality to quantity; and that this impacts disadvantaged young people by the greatest amount. Also, in Stewart, K., Waldfogel, J., *Closing Gaps Early: The role of early years policy in promoting social mobility in England*, The Sutton Trust, September 2017, the authors discuss the tensions between quantity and

quality of childcare and argue that quantity has come at the expense of quality. The following also report frames the debate around early years education in terms of quality and quantity, explains where tensions arise and describes how policies have pivoted towards quantity: Archer, N., Merrick, B., 2020, 'Getting the Balance Right: Quality and quantity in early education & childcare', The Sutton Trust, July, 2020. *Report from the Independent Commission on Social Mobility*, 2009, also highlights these two aspects of early years provision, and notes the importance of quality for underprivileged young children.

28 – The Sutton Trust, *Mobility Manifesto*, 2019.

29 – www.mckinsey.com/industries/social-sector/our-insights/how-artificial-intelligence-will-impact-k-12-teachers (viewed on 9th November 2020).

30 – Cullinane, C., Montacute, R., 2018, 'Access to Advantage: The influence of schools and place on admissions to top universities', The Sutton Trust, December 2018.

31 – Ibid.

32 – Teach First, 2017, *Impossible? Social Mobility and the Seemingly Unbreakable Class Ceiling,* viewed at www.teachfirst.org.uk/sites/default/files/2017-08/Teach-First-Impossible-Policy-Report.pdf.

33 – www.officeforstudents.org.uk/media/536f4e79-4e32-4db0-a8a2-66eb4e2b530b/raising-attainment-in-schools-and-colleges-to-widen-participation-ofs-topic-briefing.pdf, which references the following sources: webarchive.nationalarchives.gov.uk/20180511112330/www.offa.org.uk/universities-and-colleges/guidance/topic-briefings/topic-briefing-raising-attainment/#attainmentks4, webarchive.nationalarchives.gov.uk/20180511112330/www.offa.org.uk/universities-and-colleges/guidance/topic-briefings/topic-briefing-raising-attainment/#linkwithdisadvantage.

34 – Teach First, 2017, *Impossible? Social Mobility and the Seemingly Unbreakable Class Ceiling,* viewed at www.teachfirst.org.uk/sites/default/files/2017-08/Teach-First-Impossible-Policy-Report.pdf.

35 – Teach First, 2017, *Impossible? Beyond Access: Getting to University*

and Succeeding There, 2017, viewed at www.teachfirst.org.uk/sites/
default/files/2019-08/teach_first_-_beyond_access_report_digital.pdf.

36 – FE News Editor, 'Predicted grades and overused unconditional offers
threaten our universities', *FE News*, August, 2019, viewed at www.fenews.
co.uk/press-releases/33563-embargoed-review-predicted-grades-and-
overused-unconditional-offers-that-threaten-our-universities.

37 – Bach, R., 2019, 'Degree apprenticeships not supporting social
mobility, *TMP Worldwide*, viewed at insights.tmpw.co.uk/post/102fpe8/
degree-apprenticeships-not-supporting-social-mobility.

38 – Menzies, L., 'Educational aspirations and Parental Engagement,
The Centre for Education and Youth, February 2013, viewed at cfey.
org/reports/2013/02/educational-aspirations-and-parental-engagement/
(viewed on 9th November 2020).

39 – The phrasing here is informed by Menzies' own language, as
seen in cfey.org/reports/2013/02/educational-aspirations-and-parental-
engagement/ and Menzies, L., 2013, 'Educational aspirations: how English
schools can work with parents to keep them on track', *Joseph Rowntree
Foundation.*

40 – Department for Education Research Report, 2014, *School and College-
level Strategies to Raise Aspirations of High-achieving Disadvantaged
Pupils to Pursue Higher Education Investigation.*

41 – www.officeforstudents.org.uk/advice-and-guidance/promoting-
equal-opportunities/access-and-participation-plans/ (viewed on 9
November 2020).

42 – Department for Education Research Report, 2014, *School and College-
level Strategies to Raise Aspirations of High-achieving Disadvantaged
Pupils to Pursue Higher Education Investigation.*

43 – Higher Education Funding Council, 2014, *Differences in degree
outcomes: Key findings,* viewed at dera.ioe.ac.uk/19811/1/HEFCE2014_03.
pdf.

44 – Boliver, V., Craige, W., Crawford, C., Powell, M., 2017, 'Admissions
in Context: The use of contextual information by leading universities',
The Sutton Trust.

45 – Centre for Social Mobility at The University of Exeter, 2018, *Research Into the Use of Contextual Data in Admissions, Final Report for the Fair Education Alliance*, June 2018. Here, the authors note the social engineering arguments against contextual admissions.

46 – Ibid. Here the authors contrast a potential-based approach with an approach based on prior achievements.

47 – Ibid. The authors discuss a model based on prior achievement and future potential, and note that the latter is not a perfect indicator for the former.

48 – Ibid. Here the authors discuss this point, and refer to the concept of 'equi-potential'.

49 – Higher Education Funding Council, 2014, *Differences in degree outcomes: Key findings,* viewed at dera.ioe.ac.uk/19811/1/HEFCE2014_03. pdf.

50 – Boliver, V., Craige, W., Crawford, C., Powell, M., 2017, 'Admissions in Context: The use of contextual information by leading universities', The Sutton Trust.

51 Ibid. And also discussed in Centre for Social Mobility at The University of Exeter, 2018, *Research Into the Use of Contextual Data in Admissions, Final Report for the Fair Education Alliance*, June 2018.

52 – Centre for Social Mobility at The University of Exeter, 2018, 'Research Into the Use of Contextual Data in Admissions, *Final Report for the Fair Education Alliance*, June 2018. The point is also made in Boliver, V., Craige, W., Crawford, C., Powell, M., 2017, 'Admissions in Context: The use of contextual information by leading universities', The Sutton Trust.

53 – Boliver, V., Craige, W., Crawford, C., Powell, M., 2017, 'Admissions in Context: The use of contextual information by leading universities', The Sutton Trust.

54 – Centre for Social Mobility at The University of Exeter, 2018, *Research Into the Use of Contextual Data in Admissions, Final Report for the Fair Education Alliance*, June 2018.

55 – Barber, M, Hill, P., *Preparing for a Renaissance in Assessment*, Pearson, 2014. Licence details available at creativecommons.org/licenses/

by/3.0/. Report available at www.pearson.com/content/dam/one-dot-com/one-dot-com/global/Files/about-pearson/innovation/open-ideas/PreparingforaRenaissanceinAssessment.pdf.

56 – Luckin, R., 2017, 'Towards artificial intelligence-based assessment systems.' *Nature Human Behaviour* 1: n. Pag.

57 – Ibid.

58 – Luckin, R., Holmes, W., Griffiths, M., Forcier, L. B., 2016, *Intelligence Unleashed. An argument for AI in Education*, London: Pearson Licence details available at creativecommons.org/licenses/by/4.0/. Report available at www.pearson.com/content/dam/one-dot-com/one-dot-com/global/Files/about-pearson/innovation/open-ideas/Intelligence-Unleashed-v15-Web.pdf . This links to the discussion on moving beyond a 'stop-and-test' arrangement which is also raised in Luckin, R., 2017, 'Towards artificial intelligence-based assessment systems.' *Nature Human Behaviour* 1 : n. Pag.

59 – Luckin, R., 2017, 'Towards artificial intelligence-based assessment systems,' *Nature Human Behaviour* 1: n. Pag.

60 – Ibid. Here, each of these benefits are discussed either implicitly or explicitly. These benefits also reflect those raised in Barber,. M., Hill, P., 2014, *Preparing for a Renaissance in Assessment*, Pearson. Licence details available at creativecommons.org/licenses/by/3.0/. Report available at www.pearson.com/content/dam/one-dot-com/one-dot-com/global/Files/about-pearson/innovation/open-ideas/PreparingforaRenaissanceinAssessment.pdf; and those raised in Seldon, A., 2018, *The Fourth Education Revolution: Will Artificial Intelligence liberate or infantilise humanity*, The University of Buckingham Press.

61 – Luckin, R., Holmes, W., Griffiths, M,. Forcier, L. B., 2016, *Intelligence Unleashed. An argument for AI in Education*, London: Pearson. Licence details available at creativecommons.org/licenses/by/4.0/ . Report available at www.pearson.com/content/dam/one-dot-com/one-dot-com/global/Files/about-pearson/innovation/open-ideas/Intelligence-Unleashed-v15-Web.pdf.

62 – Barber, M, Hill, P., *Preparing for a Renaissance in Assessment*, Pearson, 2014. Licence details available at creativecommons.org/licenses/

by/3.0/. Report available at www.pearson.com/content/dam/one-dot-com/one-dot-com/global/Files/about-pearson/innovation/open-ideas/PreparingforaRenaissanceinAssessment.pdf.

63 – Luckin, R., Holmes, W., Griffiths, M,. Forcier, L. B., 2016, *Intelligence Unleashed. An argument for AI in Education*, London: Pearson. Licence details available at creativecommons.org/licenses/by/4.0/ . Report available at www.pearson.com/content/dam/one-dot-com/one-dot-com/global/Files/about-pearson/innovation/open-ideas/Intelligence-Unleashed-v15-Web.pdf. The authors state that AI assessments could 'shape learning'.

64 -Seldon, A., 2018, *The Fourth Education Revolution: Will Artificial Intelligence liberate or infantilise humanity*, The University of Buckingham Press.

65 – A related argument is made in Luckin, R., 2017, 'Towards artificial intelligence-based assessment systems', *Nature Human Behaviour* – although I am not referring just to coaching for exams but to some potential exam technique premium conferred generally by the type of education someone receives, or perhaps by parentally facilitated attitudes towards exams.

66 – Luckin, R., 'Grammar schools: can Artificial Intelligence create a fairer way to assess children?', *IOE London Blog*, September 2016, viewed at ioelondonblog.wordpress.com/2016/09/16/grammar-schools-can-artificial-intelligence-create-a-fairer-way-to-assess-children/.

67 – Seldon, A., 2018, *The Fourth Education Revolution: Will Artificial Intelligence liberate or infantilise humanity*, The University of Buckingham Press. This argument was originally put forward here. My interest is in breaking down and substantiating the argument. Also acknowledging that Barber, M, Hill, P., *Preparing for a Renaissance in Assessment*, Pearson, 2014. Licence details available at creativecommons.org/licenses/by/3.0/. Report available at www.pearson.com/content/dam/one-dot-com/one-dot-com/global/Files/about-pearson/innovation/open-ideas/PreparingforaRenaissanceinAssessment.pdf use similar language in explaining that technologies can be used to assess the 'full spectrum of abilities'.

68 – www.gov.uk/government/speeches/hmci-commentary-curriculum-and-the-new-education-inspection-framework (viewed on 10 November 2020).

69 – Roberts, J., 'Curriculum 'skewed by tables and targets', *tes*, September 2018.

70 – Emler, T.E., Zhao, Y., Deng, J., Yin, D., Wang, Y., 'Side Effects of Large-Scale Assessments in Education', *ECNU Review of Education*. 2019;2(3):279-296. doi:10.1177/2096531119878964.

71 – Ibid.

72 – Seldon, A., 2018, *The Fourth Education Revolution: Will Artificial Intelligence liberate or infantilise humanity*, The University of Buckingham Press. Seldon argues that academic subjects and the passing of exams are necessary but not sufficient for a quality education.

73 – Clark, J., Kashefpakdel, E., Newton, O., 2018, 'Joint Dialogue: How are Schools Developing Real Employability Skills', *Education and Employers*, November 2018, viewed at www.educationandemployers.org/research/joint-dialogue/.

74 – Hutchings, M., 2015, 'Exam Factories: The impact of accountability measures on children and young people', *National Union of Teachers*, viewed at www.basw.co.uk/system/files/resources/basw_112157-4_0.pdf.

75 – Seldon, A., 2018, *The Fourth Education Revolution: Will Artificial Intelligence liberate or infantilise humanity*, The University of Buckingham Press.

76 – www.educationandemployers.org/news-and-events/social-mobility-stagnates-according-to-social-mobility-commission-is-there-more-that-can-be-done-in-primary-schools-to-change-this/ (viewed on 10 November 2020).

77 – www.ssatuk.co.uk/blog/closing-the-attainment-gap-requires-dealing-with-inequalities-outside-school-as-well-as-those-inside/ (viewed on 10 November 2020).

78 – As already noted, Professor Rose Luckin has discussed how AI could be used to assess collaboration and resilience; also, already noted in the case of Gweek, AI can be used to assess and support communication.

79 – Seldon, A., 2018, *The Fourth Education Revolution: Will Artificial Intelligence liberate or infantilise humanity*, University of Buckingham Press.

Chapter 7

1 – Williams, O., 'Carl Benedikt Frey: Covid-19 Will Accelerate Automation', *The New Statesman*, September 2020, viewed at www.newstatesman.com/spotlight/coronavirus/2020/09/carl-benedikt-frey-covid-19-will-accelerate-automation.

2 – www.pwc.co.uk/services/economics/insights/the-impact-of-automation-on-jobs.html.

3 – The World Economic Forum, 2020, *The Global Social Mobility Report 2020 Equality, Opportunity and a New Economic Imperative*. Note that this report discusses the fact that automation is likely to increase the need for lifelong learning; the report also notes that technology can be an enabler of lifelong learning.

4 – The Boston Consulting Group and The Sutton Trust, 2017, *The State of Social Mobility in the UK*, July 2017.

5 – www.timeshighereducation.com/world-university-rankings/open-university#survey-answer.

6 – www.open.ac.uk/blogs/History-of-the-OU/?p=3040.

7 – www.open.ac.uk/courses/what-is-distance-learning/study (viewed on 6 November 2020).

8 –The phrase 'rich tapestry' has been used elsewhere to describe lifelong learning; for instance, www.tes.com/news/why-functioning-civil-society-needs-adult-education and publications.parliament.uk/pa/cm199899/cmselect/cmeduemp/57/57ap15.htm.

9 – www.mcgill.ca/maut/current-issues/moocs/history (viewed on 6 November 2020).

10 – Seldon, A., 2018, *The Fourth Education Revolution: Will Artificial Intelligence liberate or infantilise humanity*, University of Buckingham Press.

11 – Luckin,, R., Holmes, W., Griffiths, M., Forcier, L. B., 2016, *Intelligence Unleashed. An argument for AI in Education*, London: Pearson. Licence details available at creativecommons.org/licenses/by/4.0/. Report available at www.pearson.com/content/dam/one-dot-com/one-dot-com/global/Files/about-pearson/innovation/open-ideas/Intelligence-Unleashed-v15-Web.pdf.

12 – Ibid.

13 – Fishkin, J., 'Bottlenecks: The real Opportunity Challenge', *Brookings*, April 2014, viewed at www.brookings.edu/blog/social-mobility-memos/2014/04/28/bottlenecks-the-real-opportunity-challenge/. In this article Fishkin introduces his theory of bottlenecks, and explicitly refers to the role of the family. Fishkin explains his theory further in this article: www.brookings.edu/blog/social-mobility-memos/2014/04/30/from-bottlenecks-to-opportunity-pluralism/.

14 – Fishkin categorises bottlenecks in terms of 'qualification bottlenecks', 'developmental bottlenecks' and 'instrumental bottlenecks'. The limited categorisations I provide (tripping hazards, bullseyes, and strongholds) do not map exactly to Fishkin's more fundamental categories. The idea of tripping hazards is linked to both qualification and developmental bottlenecks; removing tripping hazards addresses qualification bottlenecks (specifically the 'one-shot' model) to some extent by providing additional and alternative developmental opportunities – although tripping hazards could be addressed without actually increasing/pluralising the types of qualifications available. The same qualifications can be moved to a later date. The key to addressing tripping hazards is lowering the stakes of assessments. Bullseyes are linked to all three of Fishkin's categories. The 11+ relates to instrumental bottlenecks in that financial means are required to intensively prepare for the 11+. The passing of the 11+ could be considered to be a qualification in its own right – one which is necessary for attending grammar school – therefore this is an example of a qualification bottleneck, and attending grammar school is in itself a developmental opportunity. Strongholds reflect the broader concept of bottlenecks; if there are limited opportunities, it is likely that those with

the greatest resources will come to dominate these opportunities by using their wealth (instrumental bottlenecks) to ensure their children get the best developmental opportunities (developmental bottlenecks) and the best qualifications (qualification bottlenecks).

15 – Adams, R., 'Record numbers of state school pupils offered Oxford places', *The Guardian*, January 2020, viewed at www.theguardian.com/education/2020/jan/16/record-numbers-of-state-school-pupils-given-oxford-places; also Booth, R., 'Cambridge University accepts record number of state school pupils', *The Guardian*, September 2019, viewed at www.theguardian.com/education/2019/sep/09/cambridge-university-accepts-record-number-of-state-school-pupils. In the latter source, it is argued that the number of state school students at Cambridge is still below the ideal of 93%. My intention is to focus on the fact that, whilst the proportion of state educated students is not high enough, it is significantly higher than what many people might assume.

16 – Aldridge, F., Egglestone, C., Jones, E., Smith, R., 2019, 'Adult Participation in Learning Survey 2019', *Learning and Work Institute*, December 2019.

17 – For example, concerns are raised in the following: sources news. stanford.edu/2015/10/15/moocs-no-panacea-101515/ and Lambert, S., 2020, 'Do MOOCs contribute to student equity and social inclusion? A systematic review 2014–18',*Computers and Education*, Volume 145, February 2020.

18 – Lambert, S., 2020, 'Do MOOCs contribute to student equity and social inclusion? A systematic review 2014–18', *Computers and Education*, Volume 145, February 2020.

19 – www.pwc.co.uk/services/economics/insights/the-impact-of-automation-on-jobs.html.

20 – McKinsey Global Institute, 2018, *AI, automation, and the future of work: Ten things to solve for*, viewed at www.mckinsey.com/featured-insights/future-of-work/ai-automation-and-the-future-of-work-ten-things-to-solve-for

21 – www.nesta.org.uk/project/future-work-and-skills/ (viewed on 6 November 2020).

22 – www.gov.uk/government/publications/further-education-flexible-learning-fund.

23 – As referred to in www.nesta.org.uk/project/careertech-challenge/ and www.nesta.org.uk/press-release/575m-programme-to-invest-in-digital-innovations-that-will-equip-adults-for-the-jobs-of-the-future/.

24 – As referred to in www.nesta.org.uk/press-release/575m-programme-to-invest-in-digital-innovations-that-will-equip-adults-for-the-jobs-of-the-future/ and www.nesta.org.uk/project/careertech-challenge/careertech-challenge-fund-call-solutions/.

25 – The following source discusses the link between the CareerTech Challenge and the NRS, and also explains the purposes of the NRS: www.nesta.org.uk/press-release/575m-programme-to-invest-in-digital-innovations-that-will-equip-adults-for-the-jobs-of-the-future/; the following also explains the purposes of the NRS: Department for Education writing in FE News, National retraining scheme to help adults retrain into better jobs and be ready for the #FutureofWork, October 2019

26 – Department for Education, *National Retraining Scheme: Key Findings Paper*, October 2020. Also seen in Department for Education writing in *FE News*, 'National retraining scheme to help adults retrain into better jobs and be ready for the #FutureofWork', October 2019.

27 – Ibid.

Chapter 8

1 – This scenario is based upon the vision of an educational apartheid described by Professor Rose Luckin, as seen in Santry, C., Artificial intelligence 'risks school apartheid', *TES*, May 2018, viewed at www.tes.com/news/artificial-intelligence-risks-school-apartheid and also described here: epale.ec.europa.eu/en/blog/artificial-intelligence-cracks-open-black-box-learning.

2 – Seldon, A., 2018, *The Fourth Education Revolution: Will Artificial Intelligence liberate or infantilise humanity*, The University of Buckingham Press. This scenario is mooted by Sir Anthony Seldon. Seldon's argument is one of optimism, however, stressing the tendency for technologies to become cheaper over time, addressing the issue organically.

3 – Santry, C., 'Artificial intelligence "risks school apartheid"', *TES*, May 2018, viewed at www.tes.com/news/artificial-intelligence-risks-school-apartheid.

4 – epale.ec.europa.eu/en/blog/artificial-intelligence-cracks-open-black-box-learning.

5 – Professor Rose Luckin has also argued that AIED doesn't require sick days or holidays, and that its cost relative to teachers could be a factor in motivating implementation. As seen in Smith, C., 'Artificial intelligence that can teach? It's already happening', *ABC News*, June 2018 viewed at www.abc.net.au/news/science/2018-06-16/artificial-intelligence-that-can-teach-is-already-happening/9863574) and Foroudi, L., 'Professor Rose Luckin: how AI in education should work', *Sifted*, November 2018, viewed at sifted.eu/articles/ai-education-ucl-rose-luckin-education/.

6 – Note, Professor Rose Luckin has also argued that some may consider AI's relative affordability as a motivation for implementing AI in education in order to save money.

7 – The idea of teachers essentially playing the role of 'bouncers' originates from Professor Rose Luckin, as seen in Foroudi, L., 'Professor Rose Luckin: how AI in education should work', *Sifted*, June 2018, sifted.eu/articles/ai-education-ucl-rose-luckin-education/) and Santry, C., 'Artificial intelligence "risks school apartheid", *TES,* May 2018, viewed at www.tes.com/news/artificial-intelligence-risks-school-apartheid.

8 – Nominet, *Digital Access for All launches to help solve problem of digital exclusion*, February 2019, viewed at www.nominet.uk/digital-access-for-all-launches-to-help-solve-problem-of-digital-exclusion/.

9 – Andrew, A., Cattan, S., Costa Dias, M., Farquharson, C., Kraftman, L., Krutikova, S., Phimister, A., Sevilla, A.', 2020, Learning during the lockdown: real-time data on children's experiences during home learning',

IFS, May 2020. Acknowledging also that the phrase 'schools closed their gates' is used here.

10 – *New Statesman* Leader Article, The Education Divide', *New Statesman*, June 2020, viewed at www.newstatesman.com/politics/education/2020/06/ leader-education-divide. This source refers to Green, F., 2020, 'Schoolwork in lockdown: new evidence on the epidemic of educational poverty', LLAKES Research Paper 67, viewed at www.llakes.ac.uk/sites/default/files/ LLAKES%20Working%20Paper%2067_0.pdf

11 – Green, F., 2020, 'Schoolwork in lockdown: new evidence on the epidemic of educational poverty', LLAKES Research Paper 67, viewed at www.llakes.ac.uk/sites/default/files/LLAKES%20Working%20Paper%20 67_0.pdf. The quotation and facts are also cited in www.ucl.ac.uk/ioe/ news/2020/jun/children-doing-212-hours-schoolwork-day-average (viewed on November 3rd 2020).

12 – Green, F., 2020, 'Schoolwork in lockdown: new evidence on the epidemic of educational poverty', LLAKES Research Paper 67, viewed at www.llakes.ac.uk/sites/default/files/LLAKES%20Working%20Paper%20 67_0.pdf. The following sources also refer to the fact that this paper discusses disparities in provision between private and state schools. www.ucl.ac.uk/ioe/news/2020/jun/children-doing-212-hours-schoolwork-day-average; and, *New Statesman* Leader Article, The Education Divide', *New Statesman*, June 2020, viewed at 'www.newstatesman.com/politics/ education/2020/06/leader-education-divide.

13 – Kendall, C., Thomas, E., 'Coronavirus: Poor pupils facing "two-year catch up after lockdown"', *BBC News*, August 2020.

14 – Silaskova, J., Takahashi, M., 'Estonia built one of the world's most advanced digital societies. During COVID-19, that became a lifeline', *WEF*, July 2020, viewed at www.weforum.org/agenda/2020/07/estonia-advanced-digital-society-here-s-how-that-helped-it-during-covid-19/.

15 – www.worldbank.org/en/topic/edutech/brief/how-countries-are-using-edtech-to-support-remote-learning-during-the-covid-19-pandemic viewed on 3 November 2020.

16 – Ibid.

17 – Whittaker, F., 'Coronavirus: AET to spend £2m on laptops as others call for tech donations', *Schools Week*, March 2020, viewed at schoolsweek.co.uk/coronavirus-aet-to-spend-2m-on-laptops-as-others-call-for-tech-donations/.

18 – www.streetly.academy/1147/chromebooks (viewed on 3 November 2020).

19 – Alarcón, A., Mendez, G., 2020, 'Early Openings of Schools in Uruguay During the Covid-19 Pandemic: Overview and Lessons Learned', *UNICEF*, viewed at www.unicef.org/uruguay/media/3886/file/Early%20 opening%20of%20schools%20in%20Uruguay%20during%20the%20 COVID-19%20pandemic.pdf.

20 – Aboal, D., Perera, M., 2019, 'The impact of a mathematics computer-assisted learning platform on students' mathematics test scores', United Nations University.

21 – Ibid, and discussed in UNESCO, 2019, *Artificial Intelligence in Education: Challenges and Opportunities for Sustainable Development*, viewed at unesdoc.unesco.org/ark:/48223/pf0000366994.

22 – Aboal, D., Perera, M., 2019, 'The impact of a mathematics computer-assisted learning platform on students' mathematics test scores', United Nations University.

23 – www.unicef.org/uruguay/retomar-la-educacion-despues-del-covid-19 (viewed on 3 November 2020).

Chapter 9

1 – Acknowledging that my language draws upon the term "opportunity hoarders" which is referred to in Machin, S., Major, L. E., 2018, *Social Mobility and Its Enemies*, Pelican Books, and is attributed to Charles Tilly

2 – Here I draw upon language used in blogs.lse.ac.uk/politicsandpolicy/ if-we-want-to-improve-social-mobility-we-have-to-address-child-poverty/, which is discussed in more detail below.

3 – Cullinane, C., Montacute, R., 2018, 'Pay as You Go? Internship

pay, quality and access in the graduate jobs market', The Sutton Trust, November 2018.

4 – Montacute, R., 2018, 'Internships: Unpaid, Unadvertised, Unfair', The Sutton Trust, January 2018.

5 – Ibid.

6 – Cullinane, C., and Montacute, R., 2018, 'Pay as You Go?: Internship pay, quality and access in the graduate jobs market', The Sutton Trust.

7 – Ibid.

8 – Ibid.

9 – Ibid. This report discusses the fact that internships can enable career progression, and that inequalities surrounding internships should be tackled head-on.

10 – Ibid. This point is also referred to in Montacute, R., 2018, 'Internships: Unpaid, Unadvertised, Unfair', The Sutton Trust, January 2018.

11 – www.livingwage.org.uk/news/living-wage-funders-and-challenges-charity-sector.

12 – Keys, D., 'Revealed: Industrial Revolution was powered by child slaves', The Independent, October, 2011, viewed at www.independent.co.uk/news/uk/home-news/revealed-industrial-revolution-was-powered-by-child-slaves-2041227.html.

13 – eh.net/encyclopedia/child-labor-during-the-british-industrial-revolution/.

14 – Thorpe, V., 'New study exposes 'class ceiling' that deters less privileged actors', The Guardian, February 2016, viewed at www.theguardian.com/culture/2016/feb/27/class-ceiling-working-class-actors-study.

15 – Cotter, L., 'Sheen: Arts Becoming Harder For Working Class', Sky News, April 2016, viewed at news.sky.com/story/sheen-arts-becoming-harder-for-working-class-10228478.

16 – In Friedman, S., O'Brien, D, Laurison, D., 2017, '"Like Skydiving without a Parachute": How Class Origin Shapes Occupational Trajectories in British Acting', Sociology, October 2017, 51(5):992-1010. DOI: 10.1177/0038038516629917; Here, the authors give examples of how people from different backgrounds experience and respond to the risks

associated with precarious working. And in Friedman, S., Laurison, D.,2019, *The Class Ceiling: Why It Pays to Be Privileged*, 1st ed., Bristol University Press. the authors raise the issue of precariousness as being central to how those from different socioeconomic backgrounds experience this labour market.

17 – Brook, O., O'Brien, D., Taylor, M., *Panic! Social Class, Taste and Inequalities in the Creative Industries*, viewed at arts-emergency.org/wp-content/uploads/2019/05/Panic-Social-Class-Taste-and-Inequalities-in-the-Creative-Industries1.pdf.

18 – In Friedman, S., O'Brien, D, Laurison, D., 2017, "'Like Skydiving without a Parachute": How Class Origin Shapes Occupational Trajectories in British Acting', *Sociology*, October 2017, 51(5):992-1010. DOI: 10.1177/0038038516629917; Here, the authors give examples of how people from different backgrounds experience and respond to the risks associated with precarious working. And in Friedman, S., Laurison, D.,2019, *The Class Ceiling: Why It Pays to Be Privileged*, 1st ed., Bristol University Press, the authors raise the issue of precariousness as being central to how those from different socioeconomic backgrounds experience this labour market. Both sources discuss the issue of rents/mortgages being particularly demanding in London.

19 – Friedman, S., O'Brien, D., Laurison, D., 2017, "'Like Skydiving without a Parachute": How Class Origin Shapes Occupational Trajectories in British Acting,. *Sociology*. October 2017;51(5):992-1010. DOI: 10.1177/0038038516629917.

20 – Brook, O., O'Brien, D., Taylor, M., *Panic! Social Class, Taste and Inequalities in the Creative Industries*, viewed at arts-emergency.org/wp-content/uploads/2019/05/Panic-Social-Class-Taste-and-Inequalities-in-the-Creative-Industries1.pdf.

21 – Friedman, S., O'Brien, D., Laurison, D., 2017, "'Like Skydiving without a Parachute": How Class Origin Shapes Occupational Trajectories in British Acting', *Sociology*, October 2017; 51(5):992-1010. DOI: 10.1177/0038038516629917 and Friedman, S., Laurison, D., 2019, *The*

Class Ceiling: Why It Pays to Be Privileged. 1st ed., Bristol University Press.

22 – Relevant examples are given in Friedman S, O'Brien D, Laurison, D., 2017, '"Like Skydiving without a Parachute": How Class Origin Shapes Occupational Trajectories in British Acting,' *Sociology*, October 2017 ;51(5):992-1010. DOI: 10.1177/0038038516629917. In this work, the authors give examples of how people from different backgrounds experience and respond to the risks associated with precarious working, which includes taking less aspirational paths; see also Friedman, S., Laurison, D., 2019, *The Class Ceiling: Why It Pays to Be Privileged.* 1st ed., Bristol University Press.

23 – fullfact.org/economy/poverty-uk-guide-facts-and-figures/ (viewed on 3 November 2020) which cites the relevant figures from the Social Metrics Commission (socialmetricscommission.org.uk/wp-content/uploads/2019/07/SMC_measuring-poverty-201908_full-report.pdf).

24 – blogs.lse.ac.uk/politicsandpolicy/if-we-want-to-improve-social-mobility-we-have-to-address-child-poverty/ ; and also discussed in Crenna-Jennings, W., 2018, 'Key Drivers of The Disadvantage Gap Literature Review', *Education Policy Institute*, July 2018.

25 – Dickerson, A., Popli, G.K., 2014, *Persistent Poverty and Children's Cognitive Development: Evidence from the UK Millennium Cohort Study*, Department of Economics, University of Sheffield, Sheffield Economic Research Paper Series.

26 – Shelter, 2006, *Chance of a lifetime: The impact of bad housing on children's lives.*

27 – Save the Children, *A Fair Start for Every Child: Why we must act now to tackle child poverty in the UK*, 2014. Such effects of child poverty on mental health are also discussed in Ayre, D., 2016, 'Poor Mental Health: The links between child poverty and mental health problems', *The Children's Society*, viewed at www.basw.co.uk/system/files/resources/basw_25921-3_0.pdf.

28 – Evans, L., 'Breadline Britain: 83% of teachers see evidence of

hungry children in their class', *The Guardian*, June 2012, viewed at www. theguardian.com/news/datablog/2012/jun/19/hungry-school-children

29 – Crenna-Jennings, W., 2018, 'Key Drivers of The Disadvantage Gap Literature Review', *Education Policy Institute*, July 2018.

30 – Ibid. They note that these arguments are made, they do not reflect their views. blogs.lse.ac.uk/politicsandpolicy/if-we-want-to-improve-social-mobility-we-have-to-address-child-poverty/ also makes similar points.

31 – Inman, P., 'Number of people in poverty in working families hits record high', *The Guardian*, February 2020, viewed at www. theguardian.com/business/2020/feb/07/uk-live-poverty-charity-joseph-rowntree-foundation; this statistic is also cited in blogs.lse.ac.uk/ politicsandpolicy/if-we-want-to-improve-social-mobility-we-have-to-address-child-poverty/.

32 – The explanation of the study is drawn from www.if.org.uk/2017/09/01/ new-evidence-highlights-serious-long-term-effects-britains-child-poverty-crisis/ and blogs.lse.ac.uk/politicsandpolicy/if-we-want-to-improve-social-mobility-we-have-to-address-child-poverty/. The quotation is from Crenna-Jennings. W, 2018, *Key Drivers of The Disadvantage Gap Literature Review*, Education Policy Institute.

33 – This point is made in www.if.org.uk/2017/09/01/new-evidence-highlights-serious-long-term-effects-britains-child-poverty-crisis/, blogs.lse.ac.uk/politicsandpolicy/if-we-want-to-improve-social-mobility-we-have-to-address-child-poverty/ and www.lse.ac.uk/News/Latest-news-from-LSE/2017/07-July-2017/Income-directly-affectschildrens-outcomes. The quotation is from the latter source.

34 – www.lse.ac.uk/News/Latest-news-from-LSE/2017/07-July-2017/ Income-directly-affects-childrens-outcomes.

35 – Crenna-Jennings. W, 2018, *Key Drivers of The Disadvantage Gap Literature Review*, Education Policy Institute. Here, the authors discuss the fact that poor quality housing poses risks to children's mental and physical health.

36 – Brewer, M., Goodman, A., Shaw, J., Sibieta, L., 2006, *Poverty and Inequality in Britain: 2006*, The Institute for Fiscal Studies, March 2006

Conclusion

1 – Professor Rose Luckin has used the term 'snake oil' in this context.

2 – Acknowledging that the term 'silicon bullet' has been used previously and has been attributed to Lynch, T. L., 2015, *The hidden role of software in education: Policy to practice*, NY: Routledge. As viewed in Williamson, B., 2018, 'Silicon startup schools: technocracy, algorithmic imaginaries and venture philanthropy in corporate education reform', *Critical Studies in Education*, 59:2, 218-236.

ACKNOWLEDGEMENTS

I would like to say a big thank you to Shirin, and to my mum and dad for all their support and encouragement.

Lightning Source UK Ltd.
Milton Keynes UK
UKHW021426130721
387097UK00006B/177

9 781800 315624